ELEMENTARY, MY DEAR

PHILIP KING & JOHN BOLAND

SAMUEL FRENCH

LONDON

NEW YORK TORONTO SYDNEY HOLLYWOOD

ELEMENTARY, MY DEAR

Characters in order of their appearance:

Florence Tiller
Lionel Birdwhistle
James Tiller
The Honourable Margaretta Ferriby-Cave-Ferriby
   (Maggots)
A Caller
Prudence Carlisle

The action takes place in the Lounge-Hall of Tiller Towers, an old country-house in Sussex

ACT I
    Scene 1   A midday in April
    Scene 2   Half an hour later

ACT II
    Scene 1   Two hours later
    Scene 2   Thirty seconds later

Period – the present

Please note our NEW ADDRESS:

Samuel French Ltd
52 Fitzroy Street London W1P 6JR
Tel: 01 - 387 9373

ACT I

SCENE 1

The lounge-hall of an old country-house. A mid-day in April

The place is somewhat dilapidated, but by no means grim. The furnishings are a mixture of shabby old and reasonably modern. There is an archway leading to an outer hall and front door, and an angled, latticed window with window-seat. A staircase, with landing, runs along the back wall, with an arched opening leading off. Another door leads to the rest of the house. There is a large fireplace with a sliding panel, about eighteen inches square, below it. This panel is undetectable until used. The furnishings include a large desk, a settee and armchair, occasional tables, a suit of armour and a large ornate pair of bellows. Behind the desk, on the wall, hangs a medieval chastity belt

After the CURTAIN *rises, Florence Tiller enters, yellow duster in hand. Florence is a very large lady, severely dressed. She looks round the hall disparagingly*

Florence (*to herself*) What a dump! (*She moves to a small polished table, is about to dust it, but suddenly blows on it instead. A cloud of dust rises from the table. Again to herself*) Coo-er! (*She looks at the table for a moment, then gives a quick light flick of the duster over the table, scarcely touching it, then speaks to it*) That's *your* lot, chum! (*She moves towards the suit of armour, flicks the duster over it, then stands back and looks at it, heaves a big sigh, moves close to it, puts the arms of the suit over her shoulders so that it looks as if she is being embraced. Singing to herself, dolefully*) "One day my Prince will come . . ." (*from "Snow White and the Seven Dwarfs"*) "One day my Prince will come . . ." (*Muttering to herself*) He won't! He won't! (*After looking down at her figure*) It's three and a half stones too late! (*She moves from the armour, looks at the clock*) The time! (*She moves to the desk and takes from the top of it a fairly large piece of cardboard on which is printed "RING AND ENTER". She is moving down* C *when a male voice is heard calling off*)
Voice Anyone at home!
Florence (*looking towards the entrance hall; annoyed*) Not already, surely! (*She is moving towards the entrance hall, but stops, titivates her hair, then looking down, decides to straighten a stocking*)

While Florence is bending over, Lionel Birdwhistle appears in the archway. Lionel, thin, thirtyish, is wearing a flat cap and a longish plastic mackintosh.

He carries a battered fibre suitcase. Binoculars and a camera are slung round his neck. A folded magazine protrudes from one of the mackintosh pockets

Lionel (*on seeing Florence, fairly near him, in bent position*) Oh!

Florence straightens up immediately. As she does so she, quite unconsciously, holds the notice she is carrying under her two ample bosoms, so that it can be read

Florence (*startled and indignant*) Oh!!
Lionel Oh!
Florence (*furiously*) Can't you read? (*She stabs the notice with a finger*)
Lionel I'm sorry, I—what? Oh, yes, I see. Er—(*Reading*)—"Ring and enter." (*Indicating her bosoms*) Er—which is the "day" bell?
Florence (*outraged*) Oh!!

Florence stamps off through the archway

Lionel (*after she has passed him*) Good-bye! (*He moves further into the room. He puts the suitcase down and looks round the room. He moves near the armour, looking at it*)

Florence returns—without the notice—and moves very close to Lionel

Florence (*sharply*) Now then!

Lionel, who is turned away, spins round with a yelp and immediately cannons into Florence, bounces off her, staggers back and lands up against the armour with a clatter. He slides down to the floor

Lionel (*murmuring*) Game and Set!
Florence Who are you and what are you doing here?
Lionel This is Tiller Towers, isn't it?
Florence It is.
Lionel The James Tiller School for the Training of Private Detectives?
Florence It is! Why? (*Then*) Don't tell me that *you* . . .
Lionel I'm a new pupil—a trainee.
Florence (*gaping at him*) *You?*
Lionel Yes. (*Aghast*) Don't tell me you're a trainer-ess.
Florence You shouldn't be here yet. Twelve o'clock you're supposed to arrive.
Lionel But . . .
Florence It isn't twelve yet.
Lionel Isn't it?
Florence No. Five to. But since you are here, what's your name?
Lionel Er—since I am here, Lionel Birdwhistle.
Florence What name?
Lionel (*flapping his arms and whistling*) "Birdwhistle."
Florence (*loudly*) Thank you! I've got the message!

Lionel Yes. (*Almost ogling her bosoms*) So have I! (*Desperately*) Look! Can I see Mr James Tiller?

Florence Oo! Eager, aren't we? Can't wait to be turned into a brilliant detective, can we? (*With a snort*) Yes, and I know the sort *you'll* be.

Lionel (*eagerly*) Do you really?

Florence It's written all over you. You're just the type.

Lionel What type?

Florence Dirt cases.

Lionel Dirt cases?

Florence Divorce! Getting evidence. A snooper; that's what you'll be! Peeping through keyholes. Hiding in wardrobes. Getting under beds.

Lionel (*aghast*) Getting into beds?

Florence I said *under*! Peering into poor unsuspecting women's drawers. That's what you'll be doing.

Lionel Well, I'll promise you one thing.

Florence What?

Lionel I'll never peer into yours!

Florence You sit yourself down. I'll bring my brother to deal with you.

Lionel (*with a yelp*) Your brother? (*Grabbing his bag quickly*) Don't bother. I'll go peacefully! (*He makes for the hall*)

Florence darts after him, takes him by the scruff of his neck and almost hurls him into a chair

Florence You'll see my brother first!

Lionel If you tell him I've been peering into your drawers . . .

Florence My brother—Mr James Tiller.

Lionel (*leaping up*) What?

Florence (*triumphantly*) Ah! That surprises you, doesn't it?

Lionel It certainly does. (*Muttering*) And I don't suppose *he's* ever got over the shock! (*Then, goggling, to Florence*) Mr James Tiller—the celebrated—the world-famous—the brilliant detective—your brother?

Florence He is.

Lionel (*unbelievingly*) He isn't.

Florence Don't contradict! He is.

Lionel Your brother! The man with a mind more brilliant than Sexton Blake himself!

Florence You seem to know a lot about him.

Lionel (*ecstatically*) It's all in the brochure he sent me. Fancy, your brother! A man who's spent twenty-four years in the Criminal Investigation department.

Florence (*muttering*) Six weeks.

Lionel (*eulogizing again*) A genius, a master-mind, who has solved hundreds and hundreds of cases which have baffled thousands and thousands of . . .

Florence (*loudly*) Mr Whistlebird . . .

Lionel Birdwhistle—er—Bird . . . (*He whistles*)

Florence As I was trying to say, I *do* know what's in the brochure.

Lionel You do?

Florence I should! I wrote most of the damned thing.

Lionel I can't wait to meet Mr Tiller.

Florence Why not? That's what you came for, isn't it?

Lionel (*putting his bag down*) No, I don't mean I can't wait to meet him. I mean I can't wait to meet him. I'll die if I don't.

There is a crash off—upstairs—and a masculine howl of pain, then a roaring voice—that of James Tiller

James (*off*) Hell's bells!

Florence (*to Lionel*) You needn't bother about dying—yet. (*Indicating the stairs*) He's here!

Lionel (*agog*) Is that him?

Florence It is.

Lionel It isn't!

Florence (*snapping*) Don't start that again! Don't you ever believe anything you're told? (*Moving to the foot of the stairs and calling*) James!

James (*off*) Nearly broke my ruddy neck!

Florence (*calling*) It's a pity you didn't. Come down! You're wanted!

James Tiller, middle-aged, large and round-faced, sweeps on along the landing and stops when at the top of the stairs

James (*roaring*) Flo! You silly old bag! If your bladder is so weak that you must use a . . . (*He holds up a decorated chamber-pot*)

Florence (*angrily*) You haven't broken it?

James If you weren't almost a lady I'd tell you I went arse over tip!

Florence (*in horror*) James!

James But seeing as how *I am* a gentleman, I will merely tell you I went base over apex. If you leave this damn thing in the middle of the corridor again, I'll . . . (*His eyes alight on Lionel*)

Lionel has been gaping at James, eyes agog, since his entrance. Realizing that James is looking at him, he gives a little wave of the hand. James automatically waves back, then pulls himself together

(*Roaring*) Flo!

Florence (*sourly*) What?

James (*pointing towards Lionel*) What the hell have you brought into the house now?

Lionel (*thumping his chest vigorously*) It's me, Mr Tiller! Me! (*The thumping causes him to cough violently. He collapses into a chair, still coughing*)

James (*to Florence*) Where did you find it, and what do you propose doing with it?

Florence (*shouting at James*) He's a pupil!

James A what? (*As he descends the stairs he automatically hands the chamber-pot to Florence*)

Florence A pupil—or so he says!

James (*looking at Lionel, then moving away. Muttering*) Gawd! I do find 'em. (*Returning to near Lionel*) Now then . . . !

Lionel (*leaping to his feet and holding out his clasped hands*) Master!
James (*gaping at him*) What?
Lionel (*flinging wide his arms*) Master! Lead—and I will follow!
James Blimey! He's escaped from the Bible!
Lionel (*wildly*) Command, and I will obey.
James Right! (*Roaring*) Belt up! (*Moving away, then returning to Lionel*)
My sister informs me that you are—a pupil.
Lionel (*ecstatically*) I am! I am! And I can't tell you how honoured I am
so to be!

James gapes at him, clasps his head and moves away again

James (*returning to Lionel's side*) Moniker?
Lionel (*blinking*) Pardon?
James (*impatiently*) Name! Moniker!
Lionel No. "Lionel."
James (*in disgust, as he moves away again*) Durrrrrrhhh!!
Lionel Surely you recognize me, Mr Tiller? I sent you my photograph.
James (*gaping*) Photo . . . ?
Lionel Yes. You must remember it. I . . . I was in my swimming trunks.
James What? (*Then*) Oh, yes, of course I remember it.
Lionel It was taken on a sunny day at Blackpool.
James You amaze me! I would have said it was taken on a foggy night
at Belsen! (*Then suddenly*) Lionel! Lionel! (*Almost in awe*) You must
be Mr Lionel Birdwhistle.
Lionel Yes, yes. I am!
James (*almost with reverence*) The pupil who actually paid his fees six
months in advance!

Lionel bows his head

(*Taking his hand and shaking it*) My dear fellow! (*Turning to Florence*)
Flo, you must go at once and . . . (*He stops and looks at Florence*)

*Florence is standing near James, holding the chamber-pot by the handle in
front of her—quite unconsciously—like a "begging bowl"*

(*Looking at the pot*) What . . . ? (*Then*) Oh! (*Taking a coin from his
pocket*) "Alms for the love of Allah", I presume! (*He drops the coin in
the pot from a height. It falls into the pot with a ping*)
Florence (*outraged*) Oh!
James (*to her*) After you have bought your "Mars bar", will you see that
a room is prepared for—(*indicating Lionel*)—this friendly capitalist?
Florence (*fuming, but sotto voce*) Look! I've got to have a talk with you.
James So you shall; after I have had a talk with this embryotic Hercule
Poirot.
James Out. (*He suddenly turns her round, smacks her bottom, then chases
her to the foot of the stairs*)
Florence (*as she marches upstairs*) You're playing with fire! That's what
you're doing! Playing with fire!

Florence exits along the landing

Lionel has been gaping at the two of them. James turns and becomes aware of Lionel

James (*loudly, genially*) You appear to be somewhat bemused, Mr Birdwhistle?

Lionel I—I—I . . .

James (*calmly*) Don't gobble, Mr Birdwhistle. You are not a sex-starved turkey. And don't be put out by the—er—exchange of—er—badinage between my sister and me. It was merely—er—light relief.

Lionel Light . . . ?

James Good for the nervous system—especially for me, before I throw myself once more into the task of turning you and others of your ilk from—and I speak metaphorically—Mr Birdwhistle . . .

Lionel Quite! Quite!

James From ugly ducklings into Tchaikovskian swans.

Lionel (*eagerly*) I know just what you mean, Mr Tiller.

James (*muttering*) Thank God *you* do. *I* don't!

Lionel You mean, turning your pupils from raw amateurs into fully-fledged professionals!

James (*solemnly*) Mr Birdwhistle, that is just what I mean.

Lionel And you guarantee to do it in a three-day Crash Course! When I read that in your brochure I could hardly believe it.

James (*muttering*) I prayed to be forgiven when I wrote it! (*Then, business-like*) To business, Mr Birdwhistle! First and foremost—you sincerely wish to become a detective?

Lionel Oh, I do! I do!

James Then so you shall! You shall! (*Looking Lionel up and down*) If dogged determination, and a complete disregard of fearful odds on my part can do it—it shall be done.

Lionel (*falling on one knee*) Master! (*He clasps James's leg*)

James (*gaping at him*) Arise, Sir Birdwhistle! And please refrain from such demonstrative behaviour from now on—especially in front of the other pupils. I don't want them getting any wrong ideas. Well, not about me, anyway.

Lionel The other pupils! I suppose they'll be arriving soon. They'll all come pouring in here, and . . .

James "Pouring" is a slight exaggeration, Mr Birdwhistle. "Trickling" would be more apt.

Lionel Oh!

James My school is not a holiday camp, Mr Birdwhistle. I am very—er—selective! Indeed, yes! One might almost say it is easier to pass through the eye of a needle than to enter the James Tiller School for the Training of Private Detectives.

Lionel And—(*almost choking with emotion*)—and yet you—selected me!

James (*moving away; muttering*) God help me, I did! (*Turning*) Out of the hundreds—I will refrain from saying "thousands" of applicants—I selected, for this most exclusive course, two others—and you!

Lionel *Master.* (*He flings himself on his knees and is about to clutch James's leg with both hands*)

James foresees this and moves away—casually—with the result that Lionel falls flat on his face. He scrambles to his feet, holding his hurt jaw

James (*ignoring the fall*) And now to work, Mr Birdwhistle!
Lionel To work?
James A little preliminary demonstration, shall we say, before the others arrive.
Lionel Demonstration!
James You have read the brochure I sent you, naturally. You have committed my words of wisdom to mind?
Lionel Every one is engraved on my heart.
James Quite a distance from your head, Mr Birdwhistle! However, what is the object of this course?
Lionel (*quoting*) "To widen the understanding—to brighten—to polish—so that the Tiller-Trained Detective is alert at all times."
James (*approaching Lionel*) Precisely. Let us now see how alert you are! (*Suddenly and loudly*) Tallyho! (*He dives behind Lionel, bends down and puts his hand up the back of his plastic mac*)

Lionel gives a yelp of alarm. After a moment, James straightens up. Lionel is looking at him somewhat apprehensively

(*Aware of this; smoothly*) You are quite wrong, Mr Birdwhistle. I was just checking that you are not the possessor of—an offensive weapon. (*Slight pause*) You aren't!

Lionel mops his brow. James suddenly holds out a hand from which a pair of braces dangle

And you'd better put these on again.
Lionel (*with a little yelp*) Mine!
James Yours! Catch!

James throws the braces towards Lionel, but well in the air. Lionel leaps to get them. His trousers fall down to his ankles

Florence appears on the landing

Florence (*looking at Lionel*) Mr Whistlebird . . . (*Seeing his trousers down; horrified*) James!
James (*going towards the stairs*) How many times have I told you not to interrupt in the middle of a demonstration? *Go!*
Florence I'm going! But it'd be interesting to know who's demonstrating what?

Florence exits along the landing

Lionel is struggling to fasten braces to trousers

James Caught you off your guard there, didn't I, Mr Birdwhistle?

Lionel (*still struggling*) So did Miss Tiller.

James (*laughing*) Florence? Don't worry about Flo. Flo is broad in the mind as well as the beam. (*Noticing Lionel struggling*) Perhaps if you removed—(*pointing to the mac*)—the—outer garment? I presume you do remove it sometimes. (*He helps Lionel out of his mac. As he is holding it, the magazine in one of the outer pockets falls to the floor. James stoops and picks it up*) What . . . ?

Lionel (*in alarm*) No! No!

James (*holding the magazine, but looking at Lionel, surprised*) What? What?

Lionel I said, "No! No!"

James (*almost accusingly*) So! So! Why did you say, "No! No!" Mr Birdwhistle?

Lionel I—I . . .

James Come, come! Speak, speak! You were afraid I was going to look at this magazine, weren't you?

Lionel Yes, yes.

James Let your fear run riot, Mr Birdwhistle. I *am*! (*He makes to look at the magazine*)

Lionel (*putting his hand over James's hand*) No, no! It wouldn't interest you. You'd find it frightfully boring.

James (*sarcastically*) A bumper edition of *The War Cry*, no doubt?

Lionel Er—not exactly. It's . . . !

James suddenly opens the magazine and looks at it

James Mr Birdwhistle! These photographs! These females! These . . . I am shocked, Mr Birdwhistle!

Lionel I—I . . .

James Appalled, Mr Birdwhistle!

Lionel I—I . . .

James (*turning a page*) Intrigued, Mr Birdwhistle!

Lionel (*desperately*) I can explain . . . !

James There is no need! These pictures are self-explanatory! (*He is gloating and growling as he turns over pages. With great relish*) What is the title of this—er—disgusting publication? (*He looks at the cover*) *Big Girls*. Very apt! (*Skimming the pages*) They are big, aren't they? (*Showing Lionel a picture*) Just look at that—er—those! T', t', t', t'! Inflation hits everything! Disgusting, Mr Birdwhistle.

Lionel You—you don't understand, sir. It—it's just a little hobby.

James Nothing little about this lot! Deplorable!

Lionel Oh, no, sir. Instructive.

James studies a page

James Is that what you call instructive? Forty-two, twenty-eight, thirty-six? (*Surprised*) Oh! Japanese. (*Thoughtfully*) Yes-s-s .That is certainly instructive. I'd always thought . . .

James digs Lionel in the ribs. Lionel returns the dig, happily. James digs

Lionel a little harder. Lionel is returning the dig, but as he does so, James, still looking at the magazine, steps back and Lionel, caught off balance, shoots well past him and almost falls over his trousers which descend to his ankles

Why have I never seen this collection of decadence on the bookstalls? H'm! I suppose most of the copies find their way to the House of Lords!

The telephone on the desk rings

(*Sharply; still looking at the magazine*) Answer that!
Lionel But . . .
James Answer it! Say I'm not to be disturbed—(*muttering*)—more than I am already! (*He continues to pore over the magazine*)

Lionel, clutching his trousers round the waist, goes to the desk, sits and answers the phone

Lionel (*into the phone*) Hello? Hello? . . . Yes, yes, it is! . . . Can Mr James Tiller do what? . . . (*After gaping with surprise*) Oh, yes! Yes! I'm sure he can. I'm sure he'll be honoured! . . . Yes, please do!
James (*casually*) Who and what?
Lionel (*with great awe*) It's the Exchange. They want to know if you will take a Reverse Charge Call . . .
James From whom, I prithee?
Lionel (*in awe*) The Archbishop of Canterbury!

James's attitude changes completely as he flings the magazine on to a chair and spins round to face Lionel

James (*almost in alarm*) *What?* (*Shouting*) Tell them, "No!"
Lionel (*dithering*) But I've—I've told them, "Yes!"
James (*fuming*) You haven't . . . !
Lionel They're putting him through! (*He has his ear to the phone. To James*) He's here! (*Into the phone*) Yes, yes! He's coming. Hang on, Your Holiest! Er—how's everything down Lambeth Way! (*To James, in awe*) The Archbishop of . . . !

As James moves quickly up to the side of the desk, Lionel hands him the phone and steps round to below James

James (*roaring into the phone*) *You stupid twit!!*

Lionel gives a loud gasp of horror and lets his trousers drop, unheeded, to around his ankles

Lionel (*in mystified horror*) Mr Tiller! The Archbishop—a twit?
James (*to Lionel, embarrassed and in a panic*) Don't worry. He—he's my brother-in-law!
Lionel (*in awe*) Your . . . ?
James (*babbling*) By his sister's second marriage! (*Into the phone*) Yes, of course I'm here, you—you—(*looking towards Lionel*)—clownish cleric!
Lionel (*babbling, awe-stricken*) The Archbishop your brother-in-law!

Master!! (He again flings himself at James's feet, clutching one of his legs with both hands. His trousers are still around his ankles)

James is in a state of desperation. While trying to talk into the phone he, several times, shakes his leg in an effort to free it from Lionel's grip

James (*into the phone*) Can't you get it into your thick skull that I'm not in a position to talk to you now? (*As he says this his leg is about three feet from the ground—Lionel still clinging to it*)
Lionel (*burbling*) Master!
James Stone the crows! (*Into the phone*) Listen! Ring me tonight—er—after choir practice!

Florence appears on the landing

Florence (*gaping at the scene below*) What on earth . . . ? (*She rushes down the stairs. Loudly*) Mr Whistlebird!
James (*into the phone*) No, not now! I am not alone!
Lionel (*meanwhile releasing James's leg and staggering over to Florence*) I—I didn't realize!
Florence Mr Whistlebird, have you taken leave of your senses as well as your trousers? Realize what?
Lionel (*babbling*) The Archbishop of Canterbury . . .
Florence (*at once very alarmed*) What?
Lionel Your sister-in-law!
Florence What?
Lionel By his second marriage!!
Florence What?
Lionel (*falling to his knees and grabbing one of Florence's legs*) Mistress!

Florence lets out a scream

Florence (*wildly*) Rape!!
Lionel What?
Florence (*again wildly*) Rape!
Lionel (*releasing Florence's leg*) But I never went above your knee.
Florence (*firmly*) Your bag, Mr Whistlebird! Get it!
Lionel But . . .
Florence At once!

Lionel picks up his bag

And follow me!
Lionel Where are we going?
Florence Your bedroom!
Lionel (*panic-stricken*) No! No! Look! I'm sorry if I've raised your hopes, but . . .
Florence (*moving to James; under her breath*) I'll be down in one minute!
James (*into the phone*) Hang on a minute, Soaker.
Lionel (*hearing this*) "Soaker?"

James (*flustered*) Er—that's what we call the Archbishop. It's his nick-name. He's—very partial to communion wine!

Florence (*sharply*) Upstairs, Mr Whistlebird! (*She mounts the stairs*)

Lionel (*as he follows her, struggling with bag and trousers*) "It is a far, far better thing I do than I have ever done. It is a far, far better rest I go to." (*Breaking off*) Rest!! Some 'opes! (*He follows Florence along the landing*)

Florence I've put you in room "G".

Lionel (*muttering*) And I'll bet it's "H"!

Lionel and Florence exit along the landing

James (*again into the phone*) Hang on, Soaker! I must make sure no-one . . . (*He drops the receiver on the desk, almost runs to the stairs, goes up them a little, shades his eyes and looks off down the corridor. Then, satisfied, runs down the stairs, to the window, again shades his eyes, looks out through it, turns into the room, looks under the settee, then—un-thinkingly—raises a vase from a table and looks under it. To himself*) No-one there! (*He picks up the receiver from the desk. Into the phone*) Now, you bloody fool! . . . Of course it's me! Who'd you think it was? The Commissioner of New Scotland Yard? . . . Eh? . . . No, of course he isn't here! Not that he oughtn't to be. The James Tiller School for the Training of Private Detectives could teach him a thing or two! . . . What's that? "Stop talking . . ." *What* did you say? (*Furiously*) Now listen, you crummy little crook you! I am not paying for this call simply so that you can hurl unoriginal obscenities at me! What's gone wrong? (*In horror*) You've *what*? . . . When? . . . *Last night?* But it was planned for Monday . . . What? . . . What . . . What . . . ?

Florence hurries down the stairs

Florence (*rushing to his side*) What's gone wrong?

James (*into the phone, in increasing horror*) What? . . . What? . . . What?

Florence (*shouting at James*) Stop "what-ing"!

James (*to her*) What?

Florence moves away snorting

(*Into the phone*) No! . . . No! . . . What? . . . No! No! . . . What? What? . . . What? . . . You can't! . . . What? . . . No! . . . You can't, I tell you! (*To Florence*) He can't, can he?

Florence No. What? (*She gives a little whinny and clutches her head in desperation*)

James (*into the phone*) Wednesday, Soaker, and not before! Too dangerous! Place crawling with suckers—er—students. It would be foolish folly! . . . Wednesday, Soaker, and *not before*! I have spoken! (*He slams the receiver down*) The fool! The unmitigated fool!

Florence (*fuming*) If you don't tell me what all that was about, I shall burst!

James No! At least spare me that! Soaker!
Florence What about him?
James He's done the job already!
Florence What?
James He . . .

Florence suddenly begins "la-la-ing" "La Donna e Mobile" (from "Rigo-letto") in a loud unnatural voice. James looks at her blankly. Florence, still "la-la-ing" jerks her head warningly towards the staircase. James looks towards it

Lionel is on the landing, looking anxiously towards James

(*Flustered*) Oh! Ah! Yes! (*He plunges into "La Donne e Mobile" with zest*)

Florence is still singing with eyes closed. Lionel, baffled, comes slowly down the stairs between Florence and James. He crosses his legs in discomfort, looks from James to Florence, then finds himself drawn into the "la-la-ing". The three of them are now quite close together, facing the audience— ignoring each other—"La Donne e Mobile"-ing—with eyes closed. They finish the aria with a flourish, then open their eyes, blink at each other, embarrassed

(*Flustered*) I—I—Ah! (*Clearing his throat and moving away*) H'm yes! Quite! (*He turns and looks at Lionel*)
Florence (*looking suspiciously at Lionel*) Quite!

Lionel is still crossing his legs in discomfort

James (*loudly*) It hasn't taken you long to unpack, Mr Birdwhistle?
Lionel I—I haven't started yet. I—I . . .
Florence (*suspiciously*) Why not, Mr Whistlebird?
Lionel (*almost squirming with discomfort*) I—I—I've been looking for . . . (*He looks embarrassed towards Florence, then towards James. He moves slightly towards James*) I—I can't find it! (*As he says this, both his hands fold over his "flies"*)
James (*puzzled*) What did you say?
Lionel (*hands in the same position*) I—I can't find it!
James (*with his eyes on the position of Lionel's hands*) Not find it? My dear fellow, surely it *must* be there! After all—I presume you had it last!
Lionel I—I . . . (*He goes up to James and whispers urgently in his ear*)
James (*realizing*) Oh, my dear fellow! (*He pats Lionel on the shoulder. Then, to Florence*) Flo, my dear, Mr Birdwhistle couldn't find the . . . (*He turns to Lionel again*) It's along the corridor; the fourth to the right.
Florence (*grimly*) No, it isn't! That's my bedroom. (*Curtly*) The fifth on the left!
James (*to Florence*) Why split hairs? Aren't we one big happy family here? (*To Lionel*) Off you go!
Florence (*firmly*) And, Mr Whistlebird! There's something you'll do before do!

Lionel (*dashing to the stairs*) I believe I'm doing it! (*He dashes upstairs and along the landing*)

Lionel exits

Florence (*anxiously*) Now! Quickly! Soaker! What's happened?

James (*at once enraged*) Damn and blast the fellow!

Florence What's he done?

James (*pacing up and down*) Disobeyed my specific instructions! That's all!

Florence That might be a blessing!

James I told him the job was to be done on Tuesday night. He did it *last* night.

Florence Did he pull it off?

James Oh, yes! He got the haul all right!

Florence Then what does it matter when . . .

James Listen! Farndale Hall is just outside the benighted village where Soaker lives! I told him to do the job on Tuesday because I knew that was the local bobby's bingo night!

Florence Well?

James (*fuming*) Soaker, if you please, is a great believer in horoscopes! Reads the damn things in his paper religiously every day.

Florence Well?

James (*snapping*) Stop "well-ing". I'm going as fast as I can! (*Resuming his story*) Yesterday his ruddy horoscope said, "Don't put off till to-morrow what you can do today"!

Florence That's why he . . . ?

James Exactly!

Florence But if he got the stuff . . . ?

James (*snorting*) Oh, yes! He got it all right. But—when he was leaving the joint he ran smack into the bobby's arms!

Florence What? You mean he's been arrested?

James (*snapping*) I don't mean anything of the sort!

Florence Then what . . . ?

James Soaker told the damned fool of a copper that he'd been up to the Hall to see Lord Farndale about a job—looking after his oats!

Florence And he believed him?

James (*fuming*) Last night, he did, yes! But he won't this morning!

Florence Why not?

James Good God, woman, don't you read your morning papers? (*He grabs a paper from the desk*) Haven't you even seen the headlines? (*Reading*) "Lord Farndale found stark naked with Call Girl in Single Bed at Chorlton-cum-Hardy!"

Florence Oh!

James And that was *last night*—at the very time when Soaker was sup-posed to have been up at Farndale Hall seeing him about a job. (*Growling*) "Looking after his oats!" Indeed! And his lordship, God knows how many miles away, doing the job very well himself! (*He flings the paper on the desk*)

Florence But I still don't see . .

James (*losing his temper*) I told you years ago it was time you got bi-focals! (*Calming down a little*) Soaker saw the papers this morning, got the wind up, and scarpered with the loot! That's why he rang me! He wants to bring the stuff here, today, and then get out of the country for a while.

Florence I still don't see . . .

James (*unconsciously coming down almost to the footlights; pleadingly*) Is there a pair of binoculars in the house? (*Back to near Florence*) Can't you see—the Farndale break-in will have been discovered by now? And can't you see that copper will have put two and two together? And can't you see that every flat-foot in the county will be looking out for Soaker; that they may be on his trail at this very moment? (*Imploring with voice and hands*) Can't you *see*?

Florence (*more or less placidly*) Yes, but I still can't see . . .

James lets out a howl of despair

(*Continuing calmly*) If he can manage to dodge the *Law* and bring the stuff here today . . .

James For God's sake, woman! You don't expect me to take a hundred and fifty thousand pounds worth of stolen gear into the house just when the place is crawling with would-be detectives?

Florence I've told you before; you ought to drop this tomfool "school" nonsense.

James We need a "cover"—a front, don't we?

Florence (*contemptuously*) A front!

James Ah! *You* can afford to sneer! (*Indicating Florence's bosom*) You've *got* one!

Florence The only reason you run this so-called school is because you're so damned vain.

James (*aghast*) Vain? Me?

Florence You love showing off in front of these perishing pupils, don't you? You've always been the same. A show-off!

James A show-off? Me?

Florence Even when you were a kid you couldn't resist showing off that strawberry mark on your backside!

James (*fuming*) *Oh!* I have always hidden my light under a bushel.

Florence (*tersely*) I'm not talking about your light. I'm talking about that strawberry mark. Even showed it to that curate, you did, just when he was proposing to our sister, Maud!

James Lies! Calumny!

Florence It's the truth and you know it! And there's another thing . . .

James Don't you dare mention the time I had a pimple on my . . .

Florence You're too trusting! This feller who's just arrived . . .

James Birdwhistle?

Florence Him!

James There's nothing wrong with him.

Florence (*scornfully*) Ha! Isn't there?

James (*moving behind the desk*) Not a thing! Mr Birdwhistle is obviously a complete moron; undoubtedly a sex maniac, and, most likely, a potential murderer, *but*—(*thumping the desk*)—I repeat, there is nothing wong with him!

Florence D'you know he's brought a wireless—a radio with him?

James Hardly sufficient justification for hanging, drawing and quartering the man!

Florence A portable one. One of those things you can carry about!

James (*whinnying*) For God's sake! Ignoramus though I may be, I *do* know the meaning of the word "portable".

Florence What's he brought that with him for?

James (*heavily*) Isn't it just possible he is a Terry Wogan fan?

Florence T'chah!

James Or it could be that he favours *Listen With Mother*.

Florence Suppose it's one of those "give and take" things?

James Give and . . . ?

Florence I don't know much about wirelesses, but . . .

James That fact was beginning to filter through to me.

Florence But suppose this one that Whistlebird's got is one of those—"walky-speaky" things?

James (*after covering his face in anguish*) Woman . . . !

Florence And suppose he takes it for a walk and speaks to the police through it?

James (*howling*) I have never heard such unadulterated b—balderdash in my life!

Florence Right! On your own head be it! (*Throwing up her hands*) I give up! You hear? I give up!

James And not, may I observe, before time.

Florence From now on you can paddle your own canoe.

James (*whimpering and shuddering*) Sister—please!

Florence No! It's no use pleading! I'm through! You can cook your own goose!

James (*losing his temper*) In the bloody canoe, I suppose?

Florence You can shout . . .

James Thanks very much! (*Roaring*) Get out!

Florence (*fuming*) What did you say?

James I said, "Get out" before—at the risk of several slipped discs—I attempt to throw you out!

Florence You can threaten . . . !

James (*almost demented*) Will you stop cataloguing all the things I can and can't do?

Florence For two pins I'd walk out of this house for good.

James (*quickly feeling behind the lapel of his jacket*) Damn it, I had *three* here yesterday!

Florence (*shouting at him*) Big-head!

James (*looking at her figure*) Big . . . ? "Big" is a word you should avoid like the plague!

Florence Ooooh! (*She marches towards the door*) I'll say no more.

James (*collapsing into the chair behind the desk*) Why am I so sceptical?

Florence (*turning*) And what about Soaker?

James (*to himself*) Now I know! (*To her*) What did you say?

Florence What about Soaker?

James What about him?

Florence That's what I said—what about him?

James Well, *what* about . . . (*Groaning and running his hands through his hair*) And the morning began so beautifully! The sun was shining; my early morning tea was hot for a change; the blasted birds were singing their bloody beaks off; and I thought to myself, "James, my lad, this is going to be one of those *better* days". (*Looking towards Florence*) And what happens? What always happens—you! (*After heaving a big sigh*) God help us—*what* about soaker?

Florence Is he bringing the stuff here, today?

James This morning, he says.

Florence This morning? And is he bringing it *himself*?

James All he said was, "It'll arrive this morning".

Florence In that case we must . . . (*She moves up stage and suddenly notices —through the banister—a figure, on hands and knees, crawling along the landing. She immediately comes down stage and, facing the audience, begins to "La-la" "La Donne e Mobile" once more.*

James (*without looking round*) Oh, God! Not again! (*He quickly joins Florence and, as before, joins in the "la-la-ing"*)

The figure on the landing now stands up and looks towards James and Florence. It is Lionel, who is now dressed like Sherlock Holmes—deer-stalker hat, long coat, curved Meerschaum pipe in mouth, and spy-glass in hand

After "La Donna e Mobile-ing" for a very short time—facing the audience as before—James stops singing and, very much from the corner of his mouth, asks Florence)

Who is it?

Florence, still singing, gives a backward jerk of her head. James turns and sees Lionel on the landing.

(*Seeing Lionel's costume—and the spy-glass*) Blind O'Reilly!

Lionel, very pleased with himself, stands on the landing for a moment or two looking at James through his spy-glass. He brings it close to his eye, then extends his arm to full length, several times

Lionel (*as he does this; happily, to James*) Get it? D'you get it? Get who I am?

James (*clutching his head*) I—I—I . . . (*He staggers towards the desk, and leans on it*)

Lionel Go on! Have a guess!

James (*shuddering*) Drrrrrh!

Florence, oblivious, is still "la-la-ing". James, almost demented, picks up an empty wicker-work waste-paper basket from near the desk, rushes down to Florence and puts it firmly over her head

(*Roaring*) Belt up!

Florence's singing stops with a shriek. James propels her to the door—basket still on her head—pushes her through it

Florence exits

(*Calling after her*) And bring the basket back when you've emptied it! (*He closes the door firmly, then turns to face Lionel*) And now! What the hell do you think you're . . . ?

Lionel comes rapidly downstairs to James's side, peering at him through the spy-glass

Lionel My dear Watson!

James (*witheringly*) My dear—Callan.

Lionel (*who—in the "Holmes" outfit—is much more self-assured; laughing*) No, no, you're wrong! Not *Callan*! Have another guess!

James (*almost babbling*) This isn't happening! It can't be!

Lionel (*oblivious*) Think, man; think! Use your brains! The hat! The pipe! (*Brandishing the spy-glass*) This! They should tell you!

James (*gurgling*) I—I—I—I . . .

Lionel (*happily*) Look! I'll give you another clue! Here! Hold this!

Lionel thrusts the spy-glass into James's hand, extracts a Biro pen from his waistcoat pocket and holds it for James to see

(*Explaining*) Hypodermic! (*He quickly bares his left forearm and using the pen, mimes giving himself an injection. As he "injects"*) Sssssssss!

James is watching, goggle-eyed

(*After the "injection"*) Got it now?

James (*almost choking*) I—I—I—I . . .

Lionel Aren't you dumb? Never mind! I'll give you another clue—and this is your last chance, mind!

James's mouth is opening and shutting rapidly, but silently. Lionel strides up stage, back to the audience, stops, swings round dramatically, and crooks his left arm as if holding a violin

(*Explaining*) Violin! (*He proceeds to pantomime playing violin, very sentimentally, and "la-la's" Schumann's "Dreaming" as he does so. While doing this, he moves down to James's side*)

James, by this time, is at bursting point

James I—I—I—I . . .

Lionel (*stopping the violin "playing"*) You *must* have got it now?

James I—I—I . . .

Lionel (*blithely*) He was before my time, of course, but *you* must remember him?

James I—I—I . . .
Lionel Do you give in?
James Drrrrrh!
Lionel I'll tell you! (*Triumphantly*) *Sher-lock Holmes!!*

James lets out a frenzied howl

   (*Happily*) I'll bet you're kicking yourself! (*And unthinkingly he gives James a light kick on the leg*)

James howls once more—in pain. Lionel, very pleased with himself, whips his spy-glass out of James's hand, and using it enthusiastically, strides around

   My dear Watson! My dear Watson!

James is recovering from the kick on his leg

   (*Approaching James*) And you said "Callan"! You silly old trout! (*And on the "trout" he gives James a playful, but fairly forceful, slap on the stomach*)
James (*again in pain*) *Ouch!* (*He doubles up and limps to the desk, clutching his stomach. He sits*)
Lionel (*laughing*) "Callan"! Ha! Ha! Ha!
James (*suddenly rising and roaring*) *Mister* Birdwhistle!!
Lionel (*blithely*) Yes, old man?
James (*spluttering*) You—you—you . . . How *dare* you "old man" me.
Lionel Well, you can hardly expect me to call you Sonny Boy.
James I—I—I . . .
Lionel (*striding around*) When I get into this gear—when I get the—the *feel* of *him*, I dare anything!
James (*roaring*) How dare you dare?
Lionel (*striding around*) My dear Watson! My dear Watson! (*Thumping his chest*) Yes, sir! This clobber—it *does* things to me.
James So I've noticed! And it doesn't leave me entirely unscathed!
Lionel (*still striding around*) I'm a different person once I'm dressed up in these!
James Then the sooner you strip down to your "jock-strap", the better!

Lionel suddenly goes down on his knees and peers through the spy-glass at the carpet

   (*Coming near Lionel*) What the hell do you think you're . . . ?
Lionel (*finger to lips*) Sssssssh! (*He crawls along the floor, peering*) Ahh! (*More crawling*) Ah yes! (*More crawling*) Ah yes! The game's afoot, Watson.

James follows him around. He, unconsciously gets on his knees beside Lionel

   (*Excitedly*) Haven't you noticed, Watson?
James Noticed?
Lionel (*excitedly*) The carpet!
James (*gaping*) What about it?

Lionel *Don't you see?*

James See what? (*He peers at the carpet*)

Lionel Elementary, my dear Watson! Elementary!

James What is?

Lionel Hasn't been "Hoovered" for *years*!

On the "years" Lionel suddenly slaps the carpet heavily, right in front of James's face. A cloud of dust rises. James gives a howl, then goes off into a very noisy coughing and sneezing fit

(*Striding away*) Elementary, my dear Watson!

James (*sitting on the floor*) I—I—I . . . (*He is overcome by more coughing and sneezing*)

Florence dashes in through the door

Florence (*as she enters*) Quick! Quick! Quick!

Lionel (*dashing to her side*) What? What? What?

Florence (*snapping*) I'm not talking to you! (*Seeing James on the floor*) What's the matter with *him*?

James tries to speak, but can only cough, sneeze, and gesticulate

(*Beginning to move towards him*) What . . . ?

Lionel (*grabbing her arm*) Don't move! (*He puts the spy-glass up to his eye*)

Florence (*turning*) What . . . ? (*She finds herself face to face with the spy-glass. Alarmed*) Aaaaah! (*She opens her mouth wide as she screams*)

Lionel (*excitedly*) *Hold it!*

Florence stands with her mouth wide open, petrified

(*Peering into her mouth, using the spy-glass*) Hah! As I thought! The teeth, Watson! The teeth!

James (*vaguely*) The teeth?

Lionel The teeth! National Health! (*He now puts one hand on Florence's head, the other under her chin, and closes her mouth*) The case is closed! (*Striding away happily*) Elementary, my dear Watson!

Florence (*fuming*) Have you two gone stark staring mad?

James (*to Florence, gasping*) Undress him!

Florence What? Who?

James You! Birdwhistle! Get him out of that blasted outfit!

Florence (*bewildered*) But . . . !

James (*roaring*) Don't argue! Strip him!

Florence Strip him? *Me?*

James Well, go as far as you can without losing your embarrassment!

Florence But what . . . ?

James He's got a Sherlock Holmes complex.

Florence (*looking towards Lionel*) What?

Lionel is "detecting" around the room, occasionally falling to his knees in the process

James (*staggering to his feet*) Thinks he *is* Sherlock Holmes!

Florence (*gaping*) Sherlock . . . ?

James Those damned clothes are doing it! Thinks I'm Dr Watson!

Florence No!!

James In a couple of minutes he'll be calling you "Moriarty". (*Moving*) We've got to get him out of those things! We'll strip him to the buff if necessary.

Florence (*alarmed*) But if you strip him naked he might think he's Adam!

James I don't care a damn—so long as he doesn't think I'm Eve!

Lionel peers out of the window

Florence You can't strip him now! There's someone arriving. That's what I came to tell you.

James (*alarmed*) Someone . . . ? Who? (*More alarmed*) It isn't? (*Looking round quickly and seeing Lionel is busy "detecting". In a dramatic whisper*) It isn't—Soaker? (*Then, afraid Lionel might have heard, he suddenly sings in a high-pitched voice*) La Donne e Mobile. (*The actual four words only*)

Florence (*cutting in*) No, of course it isn't Soa . . .

James quickly covers her mouth with his hand, then immediately gives a yelp of pain. Florence has bitten his hand

(*Ignoring his anguish*) He hasn't got a Rolls Royce, has he?

James (*forgetting his hand*) A Rolls Royce, Soa . . . ?

Florence puts her hand over James's mouth. He immediately bites it. Florence gives a yelp of pain. They each shake a hand in pain

Florence Has he?

James Rolls Royce? His last daring get-away he had to make on roller skates.

Florence Then it must be one of the pupils.

James Our pupils don't arrive in Rolls Royces! They think they're in luck if they manage to hitch a lift on a passing manure cart!

Lionel, who has been peering out of the window, now comes quickly down to James

Lionel My dear Watson . . .

James (*whimpering*) Oh, God.

Lionel I have just detected a magnificent Rolls Royce coming slowly up your drive!

James That phenomenon was detected ten minutes ago! Slowly, did you say? It must be very slow. Our drive is very brief. Why slowly, I wonder?

Lionel Elementary, my dear Watson! It's being pushed.

James *Pushed?*

Lionel My theory is—its big end has gone.

Florence (*mystified*) Big end . . . ?

Lionel (*looking at her posterior*) You should know what a big end is!

Florence Ooh!

Lionel It's being pushed by a little fellow with dark hair, a villainous expression and a boil on the back of his neck.

James
Florence *Soak . . . ! !* } *Speaking together*

They both clap a hand over the other's mouth, and immediately give a yelp of pain

Lionel (*continuing*) He was obviously born in Manchester.

James (*gaping at him*) In . . . ?

Lionel And his grandfather couldn't stand Gorgonzola cheese.

James (*as before*) His—grandfather . . . ?

Lionel I have not yet deduced whether his mother was, or was not, in the *Folies Bergère*——

James (*almost bursting*) What?

Lionel —but in one minute, I will! (*And with his spy-glass up, he marches smartly out through the archway*)

Lionel exits

Florence (*fuming*) James!

James (*likewise*) He's up the pole! (*Striding up and down*) He's up the bloody pole!

Florence Why don't you throw him out?

James (*bawling*) He's *gone* out!

Florence (*likewise*) When he comes back!

James (*suddenly*) Wait! Something occurs to me! Perhaps our Mr Birdwhistle is—a blessing in disguise! Ha! (*Very pleased with himself*) I like that—a blessing in disguise! (*To Florence*) Get it? Birdwhistle—a blessing in disguise!

It is obvious from Florence's stony expression that she does not "get it"

(*With a wail*) Stone the crows! He's *in* disguise, isn't he?

Florence But how does that make him a blessing?

James Elementary, my dear Wat . . . Oh, God! He's got me at it now! If that *is* Soaker out there and he sees Birdwhistle, dressed as he is, it'll scare the pants off him. He'll push that Rolls Royce down the drive a damn sight quicker than he pushed it up!

Florence (*moving to the desk*) It can't be Soaker. It must be a pupil. (*She picks up a piece of paper*) Who else are we expecting? (*Consulting the paper*) Miss Prudence Carlisle . . .

James With a villainous expression, and a boil on her neck! That *would* be my luck! Who's the other one?

Florence (*reading*) Mr St John White-Browne-White.

James (*grunting*) Lousy colour scheme! Still! Let's hope it is Mr—er—White-Browne-White!

Lionel enters. He stands just inside the archway and announces, butler-fashion

Lionel (*announcing*) The Honourable Miss Margaretta Ferriby-Cave-Ferriby!

James (*gaping*) What the hell . . . ?

After the slightest pause, The Honourable Miss Margaretta Ferriby-Cave-Ferriby enters into the archway. She is a plumpish schoolgirl of about fifteen, wearing a very battered straw hat with a tatty school-colours band round it; steel-rimmed glasses on her pimpled face; two pigtails; a gym-slip; extremely wrinkled black stockings and filthy shoes. She has a large duffle-bag on one shoulder

Florence (*when she can speak*) What on earth . . . ?

James (*to Lionel, furiously*) You—you—you . . . ! And you call yourself a . . . (*He is almost inarticulate*) So much for your powers of detection! Couldn't you see . . . ? (*He pulls himself together, moves to Margaretta and towers over her*) You have made a slight mistake, my child. St Trinian's is further down the road—the second turning on the left!

Margaretta (*quickly, phlegmatically*) Belt up!

Florence *Oh!!*

Lionel sniggers

James (*unbelievingly*) *What* did you say?

Margaretta You 'eard! (*She swings the duffle-bag off her shoulder straight on to James's foot*)

James reacts

This is the James Tiller School for the Training of Private Detectives, isn't it?

James (*seething*) It is!

Margaretta Well, where is he?

James Where is who—er—whom?

Margaretta Jimmy.

James I—I—I . . . (*With dignity*) Mr James Tiller stands before you!

Margaretta You?

James Me.

Margaretta (*after looking him up and down*) Gawd's strewth!

James (*speechless*) I—I—I . . .

Margaretta (*philosophically*) Still—it takes all sorts to make a world, doesn't it?

James I—I . . . (*Pulling himself together*) But—who are you? What are you? One might almost ask, "*Why* are you?" I mean—you're not Miss Prudence Carlisle.

Margaretta I know that.

James You're not Mr St John White-Browne-White.

Lionel Sounds like an order at the bakers.

Margaretta Your—(*pointing to Lionel*)—gamekeeper's told you who I am.

Lionel reacts

I'm Margaretta Ferriby-Cave-Ferriby.

James Margar . . .

Margaretta Known to my friends as "Maggots".

James (*gaping at her*) You—have *friends*?

Margaretta (*suddenly*) Ooh! The car—it'd better go home—before they miss it! (*To Lionel*) Gamekeeper, tell the chauffeur to . . .

Lionel To what? Carry on pushing?

Lionel exits through the archway

The telephone rings

James (*to Florence*) Answer that—and the answer's "No".

Florence goes to the desk and answers the phone during the following dialogue

(*To Margaretta, firmly*) Now listen to me, Miss Maggots! You have no business here.

Margaretta Any reason why I *shouldn't* learn to be a detective?

James (*after gulping*) I can think of several; but the one which strikes me right between the eyes is—you haven't paid any fees.

Margaretta (*laconically*) Yes, I have. 'Least, my brother's paid 'em for me.

James (*gaping*) Your—brother?

Margaretta Yes! St John White-Browne-White.

James (*flummoxed*) Your brother—Mr St John W-B-W? But you say your *name* is Ferriby-Cave-Ferriby?

Margaretta (*laconically*) 'S'right!

James But . . .

Margaretta And his is White-Browne-White.

James I—I—I . . . (*He clutches his head and moves away*)

Florence comes down to James from the desk

Florence That was Miss Carlisle on the phone.

James (*dazedly*) Miss Carlisle-Cave-Ferriby . . .

Florence She's been delayed. Won't arrive for another hour, she's looking forward to meeting you.

James (*with eyes turned balefully on Margaretta*) I shall most likely greet her in a strait-jacket! (*He shudders violently, then pulls himself together. With eyes still on Margaretta he squares his shoulders. Muttering*) "Once more unto the breach, dear friends!" (*He is approaching Margaretta, apprehensively, then his eyes fall on Lionel*)

Lionel enters through the arch

(*Almost pathetically*) Er—my dear—Holmes! This child . . . There's a slight mystery of—er—lineage. Would you care to solve it? (*Weakly*) It's—quite elementary! (*He totters away, holding his head*)

In the distance there is the sound of an approaching noisy car. Lionel comes near Margaretta

Lionel (*to James*) My dear Watson, the mystery is already solved!

James (*wildly*) Drrrh!!

Lionel You see, Miss Ferriby-Cave-Ferriby . . .

James For God's sake call her "Maggots".

The noise of the car grows louder

Margaretta (*suddenly tugging at Lionel's sleeve; anxiously*) Is that a car coming here?

Lionel What?

Margaretta Look and see, will you?

Lionel (*blinking*) With pleasure! Expecting friends? (*He moves up to the window and peers out*)

James (*to Margaretta; firmly*) Now, listen to me, Miss Maggots . . .

Margaretta (*to James, sharply*) Pipe down, you. (*To Lionel, anxiously*) Is it?

James (*more firmly*) Now listen to me, Miss Cave-Maggots . . .

Lionel (*answering Margaretta as he looks out of the window*) It's coming here, all right; just turning into the drive; a red sports car, with the hood up.

James (*as before*) Now listen to me, Miss . . .

Margaretta (*very alarmed*) Jimmy—where can I hide?

James (*babbling*) What, what, what, what?

Margaretta *Hide!* (*She looks round quickly, then rushes behind the desk and dives into the knee-hole*)

James (*seeing this*) What, what, what, what?

Margaretta (*poking her head through the front of the knee-hole*) It's my brother!

A distinctive, noisy motor horn is heard

Florence (*to Margaretta*) What? What?

James (*to Florence*) Stop "what-ing"! (*To Margaretta*) What, what, what, what?

Margaretta (*excitedly*) If he comes in, kick him in the stomach and throw him out!

James What, what, what?

Margaretta He's a homicidal maniac!

James *What?*

Margaretta We always keep him locked up between Derby Day and the Caesarawitch!

Florence gives a scream

He must have escaped!

Florence Escaped! James!!

Margaretta He'll tear this place to pieces!

There is a screech of brakes outside

Lionel (*at the window, looking out*) He's here!

Florence (*wildly*) Is he coming in?

Lionel No. He's getting out!

Florence James! The door! Lock it! Bolt it! Bar it!

Lionel (*still looking out of the window; in great surprise*) *Good Lord!*

James (*to Florence*) Lock, bolt, bar my own door against a puny homicidal maniac! Never!

Florence But, James . . . !

James *Never!*

Lionel rushes down to James's side

Lionel (*im great excitement*) Listen!

James (*grandly*) Don't add your cowardly pleas to hers.

Lionel (*desperately*) But, listen . . . !

James waves him aside grandly and moves above the archway

James I am about to give a demonstration, Birdwhistle! You will pay attention; you will mark, learn and inwardly digest; you will watch my every move; note my economy of action as I demonstrate, for your benefit, the James Tiller method of dealing with homicidal maniacs! (*He raises his hands above his head*)

Lionel (*more desperately*) But, listen . . .

There is the slam of a door off

James Now for it!

After a moment's pause, a Nun appears in the archway—moving quickly. As "she" moves past James, he, blindly grabs her

Immediately, there is a tussle in which James and the Nun fall to the floor. There is a flurry of "habit" as they roll over and over each other. Florence screams loudly. After the tussle the Nun breaks loose, rises to her feet—as does James

(*Realizing with whom he has been struggling*) Aaaaah!

The Nun puts into James's hand a pair of somewhat gaudy male underpants which she has had screwed up in her hand, and dashes off through the arch

(*Completely bewildered*) What—what—what . . . ? (*Then with a roar as he looks at the underpants*) Good God! They're mine!!

Florence (*with a scream as she moves nearer James*) *What?*

James (*unbelievingly*) Mine! *Mine!* (*Then with a yelp of sheer panic*) My God! What else has she taken? (*He pulls the front of his trousers away from his body and is about to look down his front*)

Lionel dashes to James's side, and, using his spy-glass, peers down the front of his trousers. He at once gives a strangled yelp

Lionel (*looking at James in part disbelief, and part admiration and murmuring weakly*) My—dear—Watson!

Lionel promptly faints back into Florence's arms, as—

the CURTAIN *falls*

SCENE 2

The same. Half an hour later

When the CURTAIN *rises, Florence is behind the desk. She has the phone receiver in her hand and is consulting a notebook on the desk, turning the pages. Maggot's school hat is now on the table below the arch*

Florence (*having found the required page*) Ah! Here we are! (*She finds a number, is about to dial, but suddenly looks round, and towards the stairs, almost furtively, before doing so. Having dialled a number, she again looks around, then concentrates on the phone. At last—into the phone, furtively, but impatiently*) Hello! Hello!

Lionel, unseen by Florence, appears on the landing

(*Loudly and angrily*) Hello!
Lionel (*automatically*) Hello! (*He starts on seeing Florence*)
Florence (*eagerly, furtively, into the phone*) Is that you, Mrs Butterwick?
Lionel (*automatically*) No. (*Thinking Florence might turn, he ducks*)
Florence (*into the phone*) Hello! Hello! We seem to have a crossed line.

Lionel straightens up warily

(*Angrily, into the phone*) Is that . . . Is that . . . ? (*Then, fuming, to herself*) What's the name of the damned place? (*She consults the notebook*) Ah yes! (*She automatically scratches under the left arm with the receiver which is in her right hand. Into the phone, after scratching*) Is that Little Scratchem four-one-three-nine?

Lionel, who is about to steal off along the landing, stops and scratches his head with both hands

It is? Well . . . (*She looks around furtively*)

Lionel darts off before Florence looks towards the landing

At last—into the phone—huskily and secretively) Is that you, Mrs Butterwick? . . . This is me, Miss Tiller—Mr James Tiller's sister Florence, *you* know. (*She looks round*) Mrs Butterwick, has Soaker—(*quickly*)—has your husband come home? Are you expecting him back for tea? . . . (*Excitedly*) You *are*! . . . (*Despondently*) In three years' time. That's a lot of good, isn't it? . . . Oh, yes! He's been here this morning. Just a flying visit. Sort of flew in and flew out, so to speak.

There is a bumping noise off. Florence looks round anxiously, then speaks into the phone again

(*Urgently*) Listen! I can't say much on the phone. It isn't safe. (*Emphatically*) Walls, Mrs Butterwick . . . (*Horrified*) No, no, *No!* I said *"walls"*. (*To herself*) Oo! She is common! (*Into the phone*) *"Walls"*—as in sausages. "Walls—have—ears!" Listen! If he does get in touch with you —phone you—will you give him a message? . . . Tell him . . . (*She looks round cautiously before continuing*) Tell him—(*hoarsely*)—tell him we want to know *if* he brought *it* and left it here this morning, and if so, where, 'cos we can't find it—and ask him to ring us right away . . . (*Excitedly*) He *is* going to ring you? When? . . . (*Flatly*) When he gets *where* did you say? . . . *Japan!* (*When she can speak again, heavily*) Well, I hope he sends you a fan.

Maggots, unseen by Florence, appears in the doorway. She has an ice-lolly in her hand. She moves slowly to Florence's side

(*Into the phone*) I suppose you don't know *anywhere* we could get hold of him *now*? . . . Oh dear!
Maggots (*as she gives Florence a sharp prod in the ribs with one finger; quite calmly*) Oi!
Florence (*turning with a yelp of pain and surprise*) Aaah!
Maggots (*phlegmatically*) What time's lunch?
Florence (*fuming*) Ooo! You little horror! (*She rubs her ribs*) Can't you see I'm on the phone? (*She waves the phone at Maggots*)
Maggots (*as before*) Yeh. What time's lunch?
Florence (*snapping*) You have it at one.
Maggots No we don't.
Florence What?
Maggots It's half past *now*. (*She licks her lolly. Throughout this scene she is calm and "dead-pan"*)
Florence (*fuming*) I—I . . . (*Into the phone*) Hold on a minute, will you, Mrs B.? I'm having trouble.
Maggots So am I. My stomach's rumbling like Fingal's Cave. (*After licking her lolly*) Who cooks the lunch here?
Florence As a matter of fact *I* do.
Maggots Gawd have mercy on us.
Florence You—you . . . ! (*Into the phone*) No, no! Don't ring off, Mrs B. I haven't finished yet.
Maggots Well you ruddy well should've. You started ten minutes ago.
Florence (*fuming*) You . . . ! (*Then, alarmed*) Have you been listening?
Maggots Yeh. (*She licks her lolly*)
Florence (*pointing*) Through that door?
Maggots Yeh. (*She licks her lolly*)
Florence Ooh!
Maggots Heard every word. (*She licks her lolly, then begins to move to the windows*) Didn't make sense to me. (*She turns, pauses, then speaks quite phlegmatically*) But it might—when I've thought about it.
Florence You—you . . . !
Maggots And—regarding lunch . . . (*She licks her lolly*)

Florence (*almost speechless*) What . . . ?
Maggots Get your skates on. (*She goes to the arch, calmly and slowly*)

Maggots exits through the arch

Florence (*livid*) Ooh! You little—basket! (*She moves towards the arch*)

Maggots appears in the archway again—the complete child—pulls a face and sticks her tongue out at Florence

(*Seeing this*) Aaah!

Maggots disappears

(*Raging as she comes from the arch*) I'll belt her! I'll poison her! I'll—I'll . . . (*She notices the phone receiver still off the hook, and picks it up*) You still there, Mrs Butterwick? . . . Sorry to have kept you so long. I just wanted to say "Good-bye". (*She replaces the receiver. During the following she moves around searching very cursorily—her mind is still on Maggots*) I'll talk to that brother of mine. I'll tell him straight. I'll say, "If that—that infectious disease doesn't leave this house at once, then I do!" (*Muttering*) No, I won't. I know what he might say. (*Then, suddenly and horrified*) Oh, God! Listen to me! Talking to myself! I'm going round the bend; I must be. And no wonder with that—(*looking towards the archway*)—that insect crawling round the place and—the thought of all those—valuables just—just lying around somewhere. (*With a wail*) A hundred and fifty thousand pounds' worth . . . (*She is, by now, standing near the armchair*) It must be here, somewhere. It must be! (*Half-heartedly she lifts the cushion-seat of the chair, then replaces it. She then feels down inside of one arm, then the other. Suddenly and triumphantly, as she feels down the second arm*) Aaah! Here it is. (*Her hand comes into view, clutching a small bundle*) I knew it must be. (*She unrolls the bundle. A very skimpy bra and a pair of tights fall to the floor, leaving a pair of panties, in which they were wrapped, still in Florence's hand. In amazement*) What the . . . ? (*She picks up the bra and tights, and holds them out, inspecting them—and the panties. As she does so, her expression changes from amazement to horrified realization*) James!! Ooh!! Last Thursday he *made* me go out—to the Women's Institute Whist Drive! The vicar was coming in for a game of chess—he *said*! *Chess!!* He played no *chess*. (*With her eyes on the garments*) What he played was "Strip-poker", *and* . . . (*moving to the door—eyes on the garments*)—if he tells me it was with the vicar, I'll . . . I'll . . . (*Suddenly bellowing*) James!! James!!

Florence marches off through the door, with the garments, slamming the door behind her. Almost immediately, Lionel appears on the landing. He is still in his Holmes clothes, but not wearing the deer-stalker. He takes a couple of long, loping strides along the landing, then looks round anxiously. He looks over the balcony, making sure no-one is around and, if possible, at one point, leans over the banister so far, he almost overbalances

Lionel (*as he does this*) Aaaah! (*Having recovered his balance and equilibrium, he begins to descend the stairs, but so alertly that, as he descends, he keeps turning a complete circle on almost every step. As a result, by the time he gets off the stairs he is somewhat dizzy and has to cling to the newel-post for support. Then he pulls himself together and strides, "Holmeswise" up and down stage for a moment or two, then turns, facing up stage. He then sniffs loudly as he looks from side to side. Quietly, dramatically*) Yes! *Yes!* It's in the air! In the air, Watson! In the very air we breathe! Mystery! Skulduggery! Something—sinister—inexplicable! (*Moving up and turning*) But not to me, Watson! Not to me! Not for long! Give me a little time—a little time—and five minutes more, *then* this tangled skein will be unravelled. (*Raising his hand imperiously*) No, no! Don't speak, Watson, don't speak! Leave me! Leave me! I want to be alone! I must prepare myself for who knows *what* dangers, horrors and devilish villainy may lie ahead! Go, Watson, go! (*Slight pause, then shouting*) And close the door after you! (*He prowls up and down the stage for a moment, then stops. Muttering*) The clue! The clue! What was it? (*He unconsciously scratches his head for a while. Then, realizing what he is doing; with a shout of triumph*) Of course! *Of course!* "Little Scratchem!!" The clue! In your head all the time! Little Scratchem! Work on that, Holmes! Work on that! (*He sits on the settee*) Put your thinking cap on. (*Almost unconsciously he takes the deer-stalker from his pocket and, absent-mindedly puts it on his head so that the flaps are over each ear. He then takes the "Holmes" pipe from another pocket, lights it with a match and immediately chokes, coughs and splutters. He knocks the pipe out—into the palm of his hand. A half-cigarette drops out of it. He then takes his fountain pen from his breast pocket, holds it out and looks at it in horror, holding it well away*) No, Holmes, no! (*Then*) Yes, Holmes, *yes!* (*He bares an arm and applies the pen to it as in the previous scene. As he does so*) Sssssssss! (*He then goes through a series of body contortions as if the drug is affecting him violently. After "calming down" he staggers across to the desk, pantomimes picking up the violin and bow, and begins to "play" the violin extravagantly. As he does this he sentimentally "la la's" "Nellie Dean", breaking off with a flourish. With a triumphant cry*) Eureka! *Eureka!* It never fails! A few bars of the Unfinished Symphony and—the mists begin to clear! (*He pats the imaginary violin*) Ah! Old friend! Old faithful friend! You never let me down! (*He kisses the "violin" and "lays it" reverently on the desk, then strides up and down—pipe in mouth*) To work, Holmes! To work! Bring your ice-cool brain to bear on—on what? (*Suddenly*) That nun! Mother Karate! There you have the answer! Mother Karate! The missing link! Press on, Holmes, press on! (*Striding around*) Why did she come here? *And* in such a hurry? Why? Why? *Why?* (*He strides around—up and down—then stops, putting his hands to his head, concentrating. Excitedly*) It's coming through! It's coming through! A word—a little two-syllable word—is hammering its way into my brain! It's almost there! It's arrived!! "Colour!" That's the word! (*More striding*) Colour! Colour! But *what* colour? (*He groans with "concentration". Then, with a whoop*) *Blue! Blue!* But what blue? The blue of a summer sky? No, no! The blue of the Pacific Ocean? No, no, no, not that . . . (*With another whoop*) But—I've got it—the *blue of Mother Karate's chin!* Of course! That's it! She hadn't shaved! Such was her hurry to get here, she hadn't stopped to shave!! (*Puzzled*) Not shaved? *Not—shaved?* But, damn it, nuns don't shave, do they? At least—not their faces! Yet, *her* chin was as blue as my Stephen's blue-black ink!! (*With a cry*) Merciful heavens!! I see it all!! The blinding light breaks through! Or course! Of course! Elementary, my dear Watson! (*Irritably*) Where the hell is he? No matter! Press on, Holmes, press on! Let nothing daunt you now! You're on the scent! (*He sniffs loudly*) What was the purpose of that visit? And why so brief? Brief, but not without purpose; on that I'll stake my deer-stalker! (*Suddenly*) Reconstruct! That's the answer! Reconstruct! Re-enact the scene. (*He looks around*) Now—"she" . . . came through there! (*Pointing to the hallway*) And *he—*(*he moves to above the hallway arch*)—he was here. No! (*Moving about six inches*) Here! Now what . . . ? Ah yes! "You will watch my every movement", he said. "Note my economy of action as I demonstrate blah blah blah!" And *then!* (*He suddenly pounces and pantomimes James's struggle with the "Nun" at the end of the previous scene, getting worked up as he does so. "Struggling", he moves towards the desk, then away from it, falls to the floor, gasping as he suits the action to the words*) Over and over they went! (*He growls and struggles fiercely*) Grrrrrh!

Maggots enters from the archway, and, without consciously noticing him, strides over Lionel's body on her way towards the door

Maggots (*as she goes*) Where's that ruddy lunch?

Maggots exits through the door

Lionel (*oblivious of Maggots*)
They struggled here,
They struggled there,
They struggled every ruddy where.
(*Rolling over and over*) And *then* . . .

James's voice is heard off in the hall

James (*off*) Flo! Flo!

Lionel is still struggling

James dashes on from the hall

(*As he enters, excitedly*) Flo! Have you found 'em? Have you? They must be here somewhere. They . . . (*He stumbles over Lionel, on his way towards the door, and falls to the floor*) Aaaah!

Lionel immediately grabs him

Lionel (*with great satisfaction*) Ah! Now we really *can* . . . (*He proceeds to struggle with James*)

James (*flabbergasted*) What the—what the hell's going on. (*As Lionel lands on top of him*) Ow!

They roll over and over

(*As they do so*) Let go! Let me go! Have you gone . . . ? *Ow!* Have you gone stark, staring, bloody mad? Etc., etc.

Eventually James tears himself away from Lionel's grasp. Both get to their feet

(*Fuming*) What the so-and-so-and-so-and-so do you think you're playing at?

Lionel The Tiller-trained detective should be alert at all times . . . (*Then suddenly, in alarm*) Oh! (*He puts his clenched right hand quickly behind his back*)

James (*noticing this; suspiciously*) What . . . ? What have you got there?

Lionel Got where?

James In your hand? (*Alarmed*) God! Don't say that you've found them?

Lionel (*flustered*) No! I haven't even seen them. Er—what?

James (*very suspiciously*) Show me your hand?

Lionel holds out his left hand

Lionel A gypsy once told me my life line's very good.

James (*roaring*) Not that one, you bloody idiot! The other.

Lionel I—I—I seem to have lost it!

James Don't play the fool with me, Birdwhistle! You know damn' well where it is. It's behind your back.

Lionel Is it? I don't remember putting it there.

Lionel backs away a little from James

James And what have you got in it? What are you hiding? (*Menacingly*) You've found—*them*, haven't you?

Lionel (*babbling*) Er—have I?

James You know damn' well you have! Hand over!

Lionel (*embarrassed*) No, no! You'll only laugh!

James Don't trifle with me, Birdwhistle! If you don't hand them over I'll—(*drawing a finger from one ear, under the chin, to the other*)—slit your throat from ear to there! (*Feeling in his waistcoat pocket*) Where's my penknife?

Lionel gives a yelp of alarm and tries to run towards the stairs. James blocks his way

(*Loudly*) Thief!
Lionel What?
James Brigand!

James rushes at Lionel, and after a brief struggle, during which he is obviously trying to open Lionel's hidden hand, he gives a triumphant cry

Aaaah! (*He moves away with one hand tightly closed*)
Lionel (*with a vain attempt to snatch at James's hand*) No! No!

James sweeps Lionel aside, then opens his hand

James (*with a yelp*) Whaaat?
Lionel My lucky rabbit's foot. You can have it if you like! (*He darts on to the stairs*)
James (*fuming*) What . . . ? Why . . . ?
Lionel To tickle your fancy.

Lionel disappears along the landing

James (*having run up one or two stairs*) I'll—I'll . . . (*Descending the stairs*) I'll murder him! (*Raging*) I'll—I'll fillet him! I'll murder him! No, I won't! The punishment shall fit the crime. (*He goes to the desk and picks up a small pad and pencil. Viciously, as he writes*) Memo!

Maggots enters through the door and crosses towards the hall

(*Writing*) Remember—to castrate Birdwhistle.
Maggots (*turning in the hallway—calmly*) Who? Me?

James lets out a howl of rage and chases Maggots off

Maggots exits through the arch

James returns into the room and looks wildly round

James (*muttering viciously*) I've got to find 'em. A hundred and fifty thousand quids' worth of loot just lying around for anyone to pick up! *Almost whinnying*) Gawd! The very thought of it makes me almost . . . I won't need a Beecham's pill for weeks! (*He gets on hands and knees near the fireplace, searching. Having searched under the rug, he staggers to his feet. Loudly*) Where the hell are they? (*His eyes light on the suit of armour above the fireplace*) Ah! I wonder! (*He moves to the armour, studies it, lifts one arm, shakes it and feels in it; then the other. He feels down the legs, then under the visor, stands back for a moment, then approaches the armour again. Speaking to the armour, apologetically*) Excuse me! (*He puts his hand up the front of the "mail shirt", and gropes around, then withdraws it*) Not a thing. Not even—a thing. (*Patting the armour sympathetically on the shoulder*) You don't get much fun, do you? (*He moves away from the armour, then suddenly loses his temper*) A curse on Soaker and all his progeny! (*He begins to throw cushions and papers around as he searches wildly*) Where are they? Where are they? Where are they? (*He gives a yell of frustration*) Aaaaah! (*After the outburst he stands clutching the back of a chair for support. At last, pulling himself together*) Pull yourself together! Remember who you are! Aren't you James Tiller—*The* James Tiller, the great detective—the master-mind who succeeded where all others failed? The man whose very name struck terror in the heart of every criminal throughout the length and breadth of the country—and the Isle of Wight. Whose powers of deduction brought Scotland Yard supplicating on its knees? *Aren't you?* (*He moves to the desk*) Of course you are! You *must* be! It—(*he picks up a paper*)—it says so in the brochures! (*He throws the brochure back on the desk and strides around*) Reconstruct! That's it! Reconstruct! That's it! Reconstruct! (*Striding around*) Now let me think! (*After a moment*) I've thought! *Now!* (*He moves to the archway*) When Soaker came in—I was—here. No! (*He moves about six inches*) Here! Soaker, in disguise rushed in from the Hall and immediately . . . (*James now pantomimes his struggle with Soaker at the end of the previous scene, getting very worked up as he does so. "Struggling", he moves up towards the desk, then away from it, falls to the floor still "struggling" and, by now, growling and cursing as he rolls over and over on the floor. He is completely carried away*)

James is still "struggling" when Florence's voice is heard off

Florence (*off*) James!
James (*alarmed*) Oh, my God! (*He scrambles to his feet, totters over to a chair and collapses into it*)

Florence enters through the door

Florence (*immediately on seeing James; accusingly*) Well?
James (*weakly*) Far from it! I shall never be well again—not till we've found the loot.
Florence So you *haven't* found it?
James Is my demeanour that of a man who has a hundred and fifty thousand pounds' worth of jewels on his person?
Florence No! And that'd be a damn silly place to put 'em, anyway! So—you haven't found 'em!
James *No!*
Florence They must be here somewhere. Soaker told you on the phone he was bringing them, didn't he?
James Yes. And I told him . . .
Florence Never mind what you told him. He brought 'em. He must've done. Why else would he come here? And he must have left them *somewhere*. (*Irritably*) Don't just sit there as if you hadn't a care in the world. Keep searching! (*She looks around*)
James (*roaring*) What do you think I've been doing for the last half-hour?
Florence You've got to find 'em before . . . (*Suddenly alarmed*) Suppose

that Whistlebird, or that Ferriby-Cave-Maggot horror came across them?

James Flo . . . ?

Florence Well?

James I suppose there's no doubt—I mean—you're certain it was Soaker —that ruddy nun?

Florence Of course I'm certain! The moment I clapped eyes on her I recognized him. I wasn't fooled by his wimple.

James (*blinking*) You—you saw Soaker's—wimple? (*Aghast*) Oh, Flo!

Florence (*impatiently*) I'm talking about that white thing he wore round has face and neck.

James (*muttering*) Oh dear! My mind!

Florence (*with scorn*) And you didn't recognize him? Ha! And you call yourself a detective!

James What chance did I get to recognize him? I was taken off my guard.

Florence Off it? You were never on it! I should've thought the smell of him, alone, would've told you. Heaven knows, you were close enough to him.

James Yes, I must admit—I slipped up there. What I mistook for the odour of sanctity was, obviously, Watney's Red Barrel.

Florence And you don't imagine nuns spend their lives on their knees swigging that, do you?

James No. I should say "port and lemon" is more their tipple.

Florence If you hadn't been so keen to show off in front of those poor, deluded idiots you call students . . .

James (*looking anxiously towards the stairs*) Not so loud, old girl!

Florence (*with scorn*) Ha! Scared they'll find you out for the phoney you are, are you? (*Quoting James*) "You will pay attention! You will mark, learn and inwardly digest!"

James (*pleadingly*) Sister, mine . . . !

Florence (*still quoting*) "You will note my economy of action as I demonstrate . . ." (*Unquoting*) Demonstrate my fanny!

James (*muttering*) God forbid *that* should ever become necessary!

Florence You say you've searched in here?

James (*snarling*) Yes.

Florence Thoroughly?

James You know my methodical methods?

Florence I do! That's why I'm going to search myself. (*Suddenly*) What about the hall?

James What about the hall?

Florence (*pointing*) Have you looked there?

James No. Why?

Florence Give me patience! Soaker came through there, didn't he?

James (*muttering*) Why didn't I think of that?

Florence (*with sarcasm*) Shall I tell you?

James (*glaring at her sourly*) "I do not love thee, Doctor Fell . . ."

Florence He may have dropped 'em behind a chest, or in a vase, or . . .

James I'll search right away. (*He moves towards the hall*)

Florence And when I've finished searching in here, I'll come out there and search properly.

James is about to retort

(*Suddenly*) Wait!

James pulls up in the hallway

What about yourself?

James Myself?

Florence Have you searched *yourself*? When you were rolling on the floor, both of you, he might have stuffed them up your . . .

James (*cutting in*) Well, *you're* ruddy well not searching *there*!

James stamps off, angrily, into the hall

Florence, fuming, looks around desperately

Florence A hundred and fifty thousand quids' worth of . . . It won't bear thinking about! It *must* be . . . (*More calmly*) Now, come on, Florence, old girl! Get a grip on yourself! Use your brains! Now what happened exactly when Soaker . . . Reconstruct! That's it! Reconstruct! I'll show—(*looking towards the hall*)—his lordship there is *one* detective in the house! (*She moves above the hall archway*) Now—James was here—waiting to pounce. (*She adopts a "pouncing" attitude*) Soaker came in and . . . (*She repeats the "struggle" just as James did it, earlier—growling loudly as she rolls on the floor. Sitting up on the floor panting*) Now! That was about it. (*Pointing*) They came up there, near the desk, then across here, and . . . (*Suddenly*) The desk! P'raps he . . . The waste-paper basket! P'raps he . . . (*Excitedly*) Where is it? The waste-paper . . . (*Unconsciously, she crawls into the knee-hole of the desk from the downstage side*) It must be . . . (*When her posterior is just inside the knee-hole, she gives a cry of alarm*) I'm stuck! Oh, Gawd! I'm stuck! Help! Help!

There is an angry roar from James in the hall

James (*off*) Damn and blast it! Damn and blast it! Help! *Help!*

Florence (*shouting*) Help! Help! I'm stuck!

James enters from the hall. His right hand is trapped in a long, narrow, cheap-looking Chinese vase. He is waving his hand about in an effort to free it

James (*as he enters*) Help! Help! I'm stuck! Flo! Flo!! Where are you?

Florence (*loudly*) I'm stuck!

James (*puzzled*) What the . . . ? (*He looks around, then up at the ceiling*) Where are you?

Florence I'm here! I'm stuck!

James locates Florence, comes to the front of the desk and bends down by the knee-hole

James Good God! Flo, is that you? (*Eyes on her posterior*) Yes, I can see
it is! (*He slides down to the floor and sits by the knee-hole, struggling with
the vase*) Look, Flo . . .

Florence Get me out! I'm stuck! Why don't you get me out?

James (*tugging at the vase*) I'm stuck!

Florence I'm going to faint!

James Before you do, can you get this damn thing off my hand? (*Holding
the vase towards her posterior*)

Florence (*hysterically*) Aaaaah!

James *Quiet!* And it's no use looking under there. I've looked already.
(*Suddenly and irritably—talking to the vase*) Damn and blast you! Come
out!

Florence (*loudly*) How can I? I'm stuck!

James Keep quiet, I tell you. And don't run away. (*With a sudden thought*)
Perhaps . . . ! (*He makes as if to strike Florence's posterior with the vase,
but shakes his head and merely prods it*) T'chah! Too ruddy soft! (*Still
prodding*) We ought to do something about all this; rump steak the
price it *is*!

*Maggots marches in from the hall—on her way to the door. As she passes
James, she gives a disdainful sniff*

(*When she has passed him, rising*) Hey! You! Maggots!

Maggots stops in her tracks but does not turn

Maggots (*coldly*) Well?

James (*holding out his vase'd hand*) Grab hold of this!

Maggots (*still without turning; very hoity-toity*) Thank you *very* much,
but, at the moment, *my* mind is on *lunch*!

Maggots marches out through the door

James can only gape after her

James (*at last*) The young . . . Ooooooh! (*He shakes his vase'd hand towards the door*)

Florence (*shouting*) Are you going to get me out of here?

James (*referring to his own predicament*) There's only one thing for it.
I'll have to use the poker! (*He gets the poker from the fireplace*)

Florence (*in alarm*) Don't you bring a poker near me!

James (*moving towards the desk, but not right up to it*) It'll be painful
perhaps, but—it's the only way. (*He is talking about his hand*)

Florence (*in a panic*) I've told you . . .

James (*holding his arm out, and raising the poker in his other hand*) "It is a
far, far, better thing I do . . ."

Florence No . . . !

James (*counting*) One!

Florence No!!

James Two!

Florence *Help!!*

James (*loudly*) Three!! (*He brings the poker down swiftly but, as he does so, he flings the other arm out wide. As a result the poker misses the vase and crashes on to his knee. In sheer agony*) Aaaaah! (*He hurls the poker away, clasps his knee and dances round on one leg, howling*)

Meanwhile Florence, on James's "Three!", in sheer fright, shoots forward out of the knee-hole. She is quite convinced she has been hit

(*Roaming blindly, and limping, round the room*) Oh, my God! Oh, my . . . ! I'm crippled—for life. (*His vase'd hand is waving wildly*) Get a doctor! Get an ambulance! Get Emergency Ward Ten! No! They're no use. They've been off the air for years! Get—get . . . (*He moves down to the footlights, speaking out*) Is there a doctor in the house? (*Then roaring, to a member of the audience*) No! Not you, madam! I don't want a midwife! (*The pain overcomes him. He can only groan and hop around*)

During the above, Florence rises from behind the desk and moves clear of it, rubbing her posterior and groaning loudly

(*Becoming aware of Florence*) What the hell's the matter with you. (*He continues moving*)

Florence You brute! You sadistic brute!

James What?

Florence You struck me!

James I didn't even . . .

Florence (*rubbing her posterior*) I must be black and blue. I must be!

James Well, I'm not going to look and see! (*Roaring*) Get a doctor! (*He groans in agony and collapses into a chair*)

Florence If a doctor saw my bottom . . .

James I know—he'd emigrate! (*Wildly*) It's *me* who wants . . .

Florence (*fuming*) I know exactly what you want, and by heaven, one of these days you'll get it! (*She moves to the door*)

James (*roaring*) Where are you going? You can't leave me like this! (*He waves his trapped hand at her*)

Florence No? Well, there's nothing like trying!

Florence marches off through the door

James (*rising suddenly*) Flo . . . ! ! (*He gives a yelp of agony, then begins to move, his hurt knee giving way with every step. He yelps with each step*) Oh, God! Where will they have to saw it off from? Help! Help! (*He continues to move around*)

Lionel appears on the landing, wearing his ordinary clothes

Lionel (*immediately*) Did I hear a cry for help?

James (*with a groan*) Birdwhistle! That's all I needed! (*He moves around, his knee giving at every step*)

Lionel (*seeing James's odd walk*) Mr Tiller—are you . . . ? (*He comes down-*

stairs quickly) Good heaven's, Mr Tiller, you *are*, aren't you? Tight as a tick!

James *(roaring)* Go away! Go away! *(Groaning)* If only I *was* tight! *(He moves)*

Lionel *(moving behind James)* But, Mr Tiller, you're limping!

James *(sarcastically)* Am I?

Lionel Yes. You're sort of . . . *(Following James, he limps exactly like him)*

James It's getting worse! *(He limps more than ever as he keeps moving)*

Lionel *(still following behind James)* Yes, I can see it is! *(His own "limp" worsens)*

James *(still moving)* I'm finished! Done for!

Lionel *(likewise, limping)* Don't say that, Mr Tiller!

James *(roaring)* *I've said it*, you bloody fool! *(Groaning)* Oh, my leg!

Lionel Keep walking! Keep walking and it might wear off!

James I don't want it to *wear off*!!

Lionel *(almost pushing James)* Keep moving.

They move around—both limping

Sing, Mr Tiller, sing! That might help!

James *(speechless)* You—you—you . . . !

Lionel *(as they move around, singing)*
"I'm happy when I'm hiking—
Pack upon my back;
I'm happy when I'm . . ."

James, with a roar, turns and lifts the vase'd hand as if about to strike Lionel

(Seeing this, shouting) No! No, Mr Tiller, no! That beautiful vase! You might break it! It's . . . *(Suddenly)* Good heavens! Surely this is . . . *(He pulls the vase, and James with it, towards him)*

James howls in pain

(Holding the vase reverently) Yes, it *is*!

James *(concentrating on his knee)* I know it is. Giving me hell!

Lionel *(gaping at the vase)* It's *Ming*!

James Ming? What the devil are you talking about?

Lionel This vase—Ming! The fifth dynasty!

James *(babbling)* Fifth . . . ?

Lionel Perhaps the *twenty-fifth!* It's worth thousands!

James *(forgetting his knee, alert)* What? What? What? *(He draws the vase'd hand quickly away from Lionel's grasp)*

Lionel *(alarmed)* Don't drop it! I'm an expert on this sort of thing, Mr Tiller!

James *(impressed)* You . . . ? Really?

Lionel Yes! My mother was behind the crockery counter at Woolworths for years! *(Stroking the vase)* What a pity it isn't a pair!

James *(alert)* What?

Lionel If it was a pair it would be worth . . . *(He waves an arm airily)* The mind boggles!

James (*excitedly*) But, it *is* a pair!!
Lionel *No!*
James Yes! Its twin brother is out there in the hall!
Lionel (*excitedly*) In the . . . !

He gives James a hearty slap on the back, which sends him limping and howling away

Lucky Mr Tiller!

Lionel darts out to the hall, still unconsciously limping

James is still groaning with pain. He is lifting the vase'd hand to face—to wipe it—when he notices the wording on the base of the vase

James (*reading gloomily*) "Made in Burslem"!

Lionel dashes back from the hall, carrying a replica vase

Lionel I've got it, Mr. Tiller! I've got it! (*Approaching James excitedly*) A pair! A pair, Mr Tiller. A pair of Mings! Beautiful! Wonderful! (*He looks into the vase*) Oh! There's something in this one!
James (*at once alert and alarmed*) What, what, what?
Lionel (*still looking*) Good heavens! It looks like . . . (*He starts to put his hand into the vase*)
James (*leaping forward*) No, you don't! I know what it looks like! I know what it *is*. It's . . . (*He plunges his hand into the vase*)
Lionel Butterscotch!

James makes to extricate his hand from the second vase, but it is trapped. He howls with rage and frustration and waves both his trapped hands, as—

the CURTAIN *falls*

ACT II

Scene 1

The same. Two hours later

After a slight pause, Florence appears, almost furtively, on the landing. She stops, looks down into the room

Florence (*calling very quietly*) James! James! You're not there, I hope? *Reassured, she comes stealthily down the stairs, crosses to the desk, opens a drawer, and from it takes a bank's paper change bag. She then moves towards the fireplace—looking anxiously around as she does so. She moves to the downstage side of the fireplace and hesitates. To herself, almost in error*) If he knew! Oh, Gawd! If he knew! (*She begins to feel the panelling of the wall. Murmuring*) Abracadabra! (*She presses a spring*)

A small panel, about eighteen inches square, slides downwards, revealing a secret cupboard

(*In satisfaction*) Aaah! (*She puts her hands into the cupboard and slowly draws out a black box. Clutching the box to her bosom, she presses a spring. The panel slides back into position. Still very much on the "qui vive", she moves to the settee, sits, and puts the box on her knees. Putting her hands over it, she again looks around mysteriously*) If *he* knew—he'd kill me! (*Almost trembling, she hesitantly lifts the lid off the box. It is seen to be almost full of chocolates. It is actually a 2 lb box of Black Magic chocolates*) I shouldn't. I know I shouldn't but—I'm going to! (*Her fingers hover over the box*) But only one! No more! Just one—for later on! (*She holds the change bag open, takes a chocolate from the box and drops it into the bag*) One! (*She hesitates, then takes out another chocolate from the box and again drops it into the bag*) One! (*She repeats the business*) One! (*And again*) One! (*Again*) One! (*Again*) One! (*Again*) One! (*She is putting the lid on the box, but hesitates, removes it, and takes out another chocolate*) And one for luck! (*She pops a chocolate into her mouth. Chewing, and mumbling guiltily, she moves to the secret panel, putting the lid on the box*)

Lionel appears on the landing, stops on seeing Florence. He watches her

Florence, unaware of Lionel on the stairs, presses the spring, and the panel opens. Lionel registers amazement. Florence puts the box on the shelf in the cupboard, and pats it lovingly

See you soon!

She presses the spring. Panel closes

Lionel (*whistling involuntarily*) Phew!

Florence turns round with a start. Lionel ducks

Florence Who's that? (*Looking towards the landing*) James, is that you up on the landing *spying* on me?

Lionel straightens up

Lionel No, it's me!

Florence (*fuming*) What were you doing—crouching up there, Mr Whistlebird?

Lionel Laying an egg. I mean—I was tying my shoelace. (*He begins to descend the stairs hesitantly*)

Florence You weren't! I know what you were doing. You were . . .

Suddenly, from off upstairs, comes the terrifically loud clanging of a large handbell. The suddenness and volume of the clanging causes Lionel to fall down the stairs

(*Seeing this*) Aaaaah!

Lionel arrives at the bottom of the stairs and lies moaning in agony

(*Hopefully*) You *have* hurt yourself, haven't you?

Lionel howls

(*Again hopefully*) You're not dead, are you?

Lionel (*faintly*) I think so.

Florence (*grumbling*) Don't worry! You're not! I never have any luck—not even with "Ernie"! (*Sharply*) Come on! Get up! You're not going to spend the afternoon lolling about down there!

Lionel, moaning, staggers to his feet. The handbell is heard again, loudly. Lionel, in his dazed condition, gives a yelp of alarm and puts his arms round Florence, clinging on to her

Lionel (*as he does this*) Aaaah!

Florence (*sharply*) Now then! Now then! None of that! (*She disentangles herself from Lionel's embrace*) You're not my type!

Lionel (*dazedly running a hand across his brow*) Oh, my Lord!

Florence (*with satisfaction*) You're in a bad way, aren't you?

Lionel I—I had my arms round *you*, hadn't I?

Florence (*snorting*) You had!

Lionel Then I must be! (*He staggers a little*)

Maggots dashes in from the hall and goes quickly to Florence's side

Florence (*to Lionel, with her back to Maggots*) Do you want an ambulance to take you home? (*Quickly*) Did you say, "Yes, please!"?

Maggots gives Florence's posterior a sharp prod with one finger

(*In surprise and pain as she turns round*) Aaaah! (*She unconsciously drops the bag of chocolates on the floor*)

Maggots (*unheeding*) What's that bell ringing for—fire?

Florence (*fuming*) You—you . . . !

Maggots Or is it tea-time?

Florence If you want to know . . .

Maggots That's why I asked.

Lionel (*feebly*) And I was coming round to that when I come round.

Florence That bell is Mr Tiller.

Lionel (*brightly*) Ah! *The Ringer* (*Explaining*) Edgar Wallace!

Florence (*snorting*) He always rings a bell five minutes before lessons start. (*Glaring at Maggots and Lionel*) Though, with you two to cope with, he shouldn't be *ringing* it—he should be *tolling* it!

Florence marches out through the door

Maggots immediately spots the bag on the floor, picks it up and moves to the door, opening the bag as she does so

Maggots (*calling off*) Hey! Half a minute! You've forgotten your . . . (*Realizing what the bag contains*) No, you haven't. (*Taking a chocolate from the bag*) Thanks a lot! (*She pops the chocolate into her mouth*)

Lionel You didn't ought to do that. You never know where they've been.

Maggots No, but I know where they're going. (*She puts the bag into her knickers*)

Lionel (*seeing this*) Don't lose 'em! (*He dashes down to the wall, below the fireplace, and immediately begins feeling it for the spring*)

Maggots (*coming down to him*) What do you think you're doing?

Lionel (*starting*) Oh! I thought you were otherwise engaged?

Maggots (*phlegmatically*) What're you doing?

Lionel Doing? Oh—er—just—just . . . (*He puts his hands to the wall again*)

Maggots (*as before*) What?

Lionel Just—straightening the wall. It seemed to be tilting this way a little. (*Giving the wall a "push"*) There! That's got it!

The handbell is heard off, then James's voice

James (*off*) Bring out your dead!

Lionel (*alert*) Look out! (*He drags Maggots away from the wall*)

James appears on the landing, ringing the bell. He is wearing a mortar-board and gown

James (*when well on the landing; roaring*) Bring out your dead! (*Looking over the banister, dolefully*) Oh! They're out already!

Lionel (*gaping at him*) What the . . . ?

James (*grandly, as he descends the stairs*) Places! Places! Take your places! Be it known by those present that the James Tiller Crash Course on the Art of Detection is about to commence!

Lionel (*pointing to the mortar-board*) Not in that 'at?

James (*ignoring him*) Using his own original, inimitable and fool-proof methods, Mr James Tiller, will, in person, and before your very eyes, transform these—(*indicating Lionel and Maggots*)—muling and puking morons . . .

Lionel (*indignantly*) I'm not muling!

James You'll be puking in a minute—if you interrupt me again.

Maggots T'chah! Disgusting!

James (*turning on her*) So! So! Hoity-toity! Have we offended the— delicate—shell-like ears of The Honourable Miss *Debrett*, *Who's Who*, and potential sub-editor of *The Teenagers Guide to Crime*? Er—where was I? What was I saying?

Lionel Nothing.

James I remember! It is my firm intention, come weal, come woe—and I suspect the woe will exceed the weal by ninety-five per cent—to turn you two subnormal morons into two highly efficient detectors of crime in all its numerous and nefarious branches—i.e. . . .

Lionel (*waving a hand at him*) Aye, aye!

James (*glaring at him*) I—e—er . . . We'll deal with the "i.e.s" as we come to them. (*Moving behind the desk*) First of all we will take the roll-call. (*Clapping his hands authoritatively*) And pull up a couple of chairs— in front of my desk!

Lionel Did you say roll-call?

James (*raising his voice*) I have to make sure you're both here, haven't I? (*He produces a roll-call book*)

Lionel quickly finds a small, hard chair and brings it in front of the desk. James consults a sheet of paper. Maggots, with difficulty, pushes the largest and most comfortable armchair in front of the desk

Lionel (*about to sit on a hard chair*) Oh! Thanks very much! (*He sits in the armchair*)

Maggots (*furiously*) Oooh! That's mine! (*She tries to sit in the armchair, but lands on Lionel's lap*)

They both struggle for possession of the chair

James (*looking up from his paper*) Musical Chairs is not a subject in my curriculum. Nor, Mr Birdwhistle, do we, at this early stage, deal with the abominable crime of Child Seduction!

Lionel (*pushing Maggots of his knee; indignantly*) I didn't—I wasn't!

James You was! (*He goes and brings down a hard stool*) If you will park your person on this, we will continue.

Lionel sits on the stool, with his back to the door

(*Behind the desk again*) Now—roll-call!

Florence appears in the doorway

Florence (*hissing mysteriously to James*) Sssssssss! (*She beckons to him*)

Lionel (*whose back is to Florence*) Is that gas leaking?
James No. My sister. *Pardonnez mois, mes enfants.* (*He moves towards Florence, then turns to the others*) That was French!

James moves further towards Florence. She beckons him closer. Then whispering in his ear, she disappears through the door, holding James by the hand. James follows her until only his posterior is in view

Maggots (*meanwhile; to Lionel*) D'you know, I've come to a conclusion! (*Jerking her head towards the door*) He's a phony!
Lionel Mr Tiller?
Maggots I don't believe he's ever been a detective at all!
Lionel Not . . . ?
Maggots (*looking at Lionel*) Well, does he look like one?
Lionel (*looking across at James's posterior*) Not at the moment!
Maggots (*mysteriously*) I'd like to get to the bottom of him!
Lionel Well, now's your chance. And you'll never have it so good!
Maggots (*with a jerk of her head towards James*) Those two—they're worried about something!
Lionel (*looking her up and down*) Well, that's understandable!

James silently leaves the door

Maggots (*looking him up and down; innocently*) No, I don't mean *you*, particularly. Though, the Lord knows . . .
Lionel Thanks very much.
Maggots Do you know what *I* think?
Lionel I didn't ever know you did think!

James quietly moves between Lionel and Maggots

Maggots Well, I do—often.
Lionel P'raps you've been overdoing it. I do occasionally. You'd never believe the—ideas—I get into my head sometimes.
James (*fairly loudly*) *What* ideas, Mr Birdwhistle?

Lionel and Maggots give little yelps of surprise

Lionel I—I—I . . .
James I await your reply, Mr Birdwhistle. (*He moves behind the desk*)
Lionel And I'm trying to think of one.

James looks at him suspiciously for quite a while, drumming his fingers on the desk

James What iniquitous ideas were you about to put into this child's head?
Lionel I wasn't! I never! I wouldn't! I couldn't!
James Such protestations, Mr Birdwhistle! A sure sign of guilt! I've just been hearing things about you! (*He indicates the door*)
Lionel (*alarmed*) About me? What things?
James (*darkly*) Your—lurkings!
Lionel (*puzzled*) My—lurkings? (*Both his hands, unconsciously cover his "flies"*)

James Your lecherous lurkings on the landing!

Lionel (*relieved*) Oh, those!

James (*to Maggots*) You must be protected, my child, at cost. (*Pointing to a rough iron contraption which is hanging on the wall*) That—contraption which you see hanging on the wall; do you know what it is—and I pray the answer is "No"?

Maggots (*looking*) No, I'm b-blessed if I do.

James You are indeed blessed.

Lionel (*also looking*) It's got *me* flummoxed.

James (*with meaning*) It *will*, Mr Birdwhistle; it most certainly *will* (*To Maggots*) That, my child, is a medieval belt worn by ladies of high quality, and low morals, when their husbands were away for the weekends. I do not propose to sully your innocent ears with the whys and wherefores, *but*—the moment this lesson is over, you would be well advised to take that belt and slip into it! (*He glares at Lionel*) *And now.* (*Picking up the register*) Roll-call! As your names are called you will answer "Present". Understand?

Maggots Yep!

James (*reading*) Ferriby-Cave-Ferriby, The Honourable Miss Margaretta.

Maggots (*as before*) Yep!

As James glares at her, she gives a small "V for Victory" sign—which could be misinterpreted

James (*after breathing heavily; reading*) Birdwhistle, Lionel.

Lionel (*with studied nonchalance*) Adsum!

James (*looking up*) What?

Lionel (*as before*) Adsum! (*With more nonchalance he polishes the nails of one hand on the lapel of his jacket*)

James is gaping at him

(*Aware of this, holding out a hand and admiring his nails*) Adsum! (*Beaming at James, he repeats the polishing business on his other hand. Very pleased with himself*) Adsum!

James (*roaring angrily*) Birdwhistle!

Lionel (*smoothly*) Adsum! (*More finger-waving*)

James (*speechless*) I—I—I . . .

Lionel (*airily*) Latin for "Present", you know.

James (*derisively*) We've gone very Oxford, Cambridge and Fortnum 'n Mason all at once, haven't we?

Lionel (*carried away*) Adsum! (*More polishing*)

James (*breathing heavily*) All right! If that's how you want it—*ADSUM!*

Lionel (*lightly*) Yes. Some '*ad*—and some '*adn't*!

James (*at bursting point*) What?

Lionel Joke! *Adsum*—some '*ad*—and some '*adn't*!

Lionel roars with laughter at his "joke", leans backwards and overbalances off the stool on to the floor. Still laughing he picks himself up

(*Digging Maggots in the ribs*) Some '*ad*!

Maggots Ow!

Lionel (*digging James in the ribs*) —and some 'adn't!

James Birdwhistle!

Lionel (*screaming with laughter—loudly*) Adsum! (*More laughter, then, wiping the tears from his eyes*) Oh, isn't life gay!

James (*seething*) Birdwhistle, when this lesson is over, you will stay behind!

Lionel (*still laughing*) With my trousers "at the ready"—I know. (*Laughing*) And when you've finished with me, I shall've—(*he makes a cane-swiping gesture*)—'ad some! (*He collapses into the armchair*)

Maggots (*wearily*) Can't we get on?

James With Mr Birdwhistle's permission, we can and we will. Er—where were we? Ah yes? (*Picking it up*) The register! (*Reading*) Birdwhistle, Lionel. (*Then with a quick yelp*) No! My God, no! Not again! (*Reading*) Carlisle—Miss Prudence. (*Raising his voice*) And where the devil is Miss Carlisle?

A female voice is heard off from the hallway, almost singing. Lionel moves towards the arch

Voice (*off*) Ad-sum!

James lets out an agonized howl

> *Prudence Carlisle appears in the archway. She is a very glamorous, bubbling blonde of around thirty. She wears a startlingly revealing dress and has an expensive fur coat draped around her shoulders*

Prudence (*happily*) Ad-sum!

Lionel (*completely carried away, goggling and gabbling*) Oh! Oh, yes! Oh, well! Oh, marvellous! Oh, my goodness! Oh! Oh! Oh!

Prudence (*holding both hands out*) Mister Tiller!

Lionel moves towards her. She pulls him straight into her arms

Lionel (*as she does so*) Oh! Oh! Oh!

Prudence (*after giving him a light kiss on the cheek*) I'm sorry I'm late, darling.

Lionel (*waving his arms*) Oh! Oh! Oh!

Prudence (*happily disengaging herself*) But you knew I would be, didn't you? (*Beaming at him*) I mean—the message—you *got* it, didn't you? (*She ogles him*)

Lionel (*babbling, under the influence*) The . . . ? Oh, the message! Yes, yes, I got it. (*Then*) Er—at least—(*gazing at her*)—I'm *getting* it!

Prudence (*moving into the room and automatically taking Lionel with her by the hand*) Well, now . . . ! Introductions! (*Seeing James, to Lionel*) Who's the funny man in the funny hat?

Lionel (*gulping*) I—I . . .

James (*booming*) Miss Carlisle!

Prudence (*blithely*) Yes, darling?

James (*collapsing*) I—I—I . . . (*Gibbering*) You *are* Miss Carlisle, I presume, Miss Carlisle?

Prudence (*sweetly*) I am.

James May I introduce myself?

Prudence Of course.

James (*with dignity*) *I* am Mr James Tiller!

Prudence (*gaping*) *You*—darling?

James Yes, darling. (*Then*) I—I—I . . . Welcome to Tiller Towers.

Prudence (*her voice hardening a little*) So *you* are Mr James Tiller?

James (*proudly*) I am!

Prudence (*looking at him somewhat curiously*) H'm!

James (*nettled*) I trust I meet with your approbation.

Prudence (*returning to her "gay" mood*) But, of course! (*She runs to him and gives him a light kiss*) Darling!

James's arms unconsciously go round her

James (*automatically*) Darling!

Maggots gives a big snort

Prudence (*noticing her for the first time*) Oh! And—er—what is this?

Maggots (*fuming*) Oooh!

Prudence (*gaily*) But, of course! I can *see* what it is! (*To James*) Your little grand-daughter!

Lionel sniggers

James (*speechless*) I—I—I . . . !

Prudence (*sweeping on*) The likeness—quite remarkable! (*Patting Maggots on the head*) Never mind, darling. We can't *all* be swans, can we?

James (*gulping*) Miss Ferriby-Cave-Ferriby is a pupil, *not* my—my—grand—grand . . . (*He cannot say the word*)

Prudence Not . . . ?

James Not!

Prudence Oh, dear! My—er—"detection" isn't very good yet, is it?

James (*growling to himself*) It's bloody aw . . . !

Prudence (*sweeping on*) But it will be! It will be! I'm sure that with your help—your guidance . . . (*She lays a hand on James's arm*)

James (*melted butter*) Ah well . . . (*Putting a hand over hers*) I shall do every possible thing I can!

Lionel (*muttering*) And I'll bet he'll try a few he *can't!*

James (*eyes on Lionel*) Perhaps we'd better get *all* the introductions over. That—(*indicating Lionel*)—is another—one might almost say—*the* other of your fellow pupils, Mr Lionel Birdwhistle.

Prudence (*moving quickly to Lionel, cooing*) *Mis*ter Birdwhistle! (*She takes both his hands*) And I mistook *you* for Mr Tiller!!

Lionel (*gurgling*) Please—don't mention it. It was . . .

Prudence I know what it was, Mr Birdwhistle. It was—(*with a quick deprecating glance at James*)—unforgivable!

James reacts

(*To Lionel*) I mean—*you* are so—so virile—so—handsome!

More reaction from James. Lionel's legs writhe in embarrassment

But you're a fellow pupil! I'm so glad! (*Slipping an arm through Lionel's and grabbing his hand and patting it*) So glad! (*Archly*) We'll have some fun, won't we?

Lionel (*carried away*) Oh, yes! Some fun! Some games! (*He sees James glaring at him*) Some hopes!

James (*clapping his hands authoritatively*) And *now!* We must get on!

Lionel (*Patting Prudence's hand*) I'm not doing too badly!

James No more playful badinage, Mr Birdwhistle! From now on we must work, work, *Work!* (*To Prudence*) Oh! But first, I must arrange for you to be shown to your room, Miss Carlisle.

Prudence (*with a coy moue*) Aren't you going to call me Prudence?

James (*embarrassed*) I—I—I . . .

Prudence (*sweetly*) Because I'm going to call you "Papa".

James can only "gobble"

Florence enters through the door

James (*seeing her*) Ah, Flo—er—Florence! A very well-timed entrance; dead on cue. I was about to ring for you.

Florence (*with a disapproving eye on Prudence, sarcastically*) *Were* you?

James (*grandly*) I was. Miss Carlisle has just arrived and would like to go up to her room.

Florence (*balefully*) She would, would she?

Prudence (*happily*) No, no. I wouldn't; not yet.

James (*somewhat baffled*) No? But don't you want to—er—er . . .

Prudence (*easily*) No, thank you. I—"er—er'd"—half an hour ago. I'd much rather—(*smiling*)—crash on with "Crash Course". (*To Florence*) But my bags; they're in the hallway. Would you be a popsy——

Florence reacts

—and bring them in here. (*She propels Florence towards the arch*) Don't bother to take them upstairs. (*Looking Florence up and down*) You'd never manage them. I'm *sure*—(*beaming at him*)—Mr Birdwhistle will help me carry them up later.

Lionel (*alarmed*) Will I?

James (*to Florence*) Bring the bags in here—popsy.

Florence, at bursting point, stamps out into the hall

(*Raising his voice*) And now—if you will take your places . . . !

Maggots rushes to the armchair and sits in it. James almost automatically takes her by the ear and puts her on the stool

(*Speaking as he does this*) If you will sit here—Prudence! (*He indicates the armchair*)

Lionel sits on the hard chair next to the armchair

Prudence (*beaming*) Next to Mr Birdwhistle! How lovely!

Florence returns from the hall, carrying two very expensive-looking suit-cases

Florence (*as she dumps them just inside the room*) Your bags!
Prudence (*sweetly and gaily*) Thank you! (*With a dismissing wave of the hand*) I'll—*see* you later. ("*See*" *meaning* "*tip*")

Florence, raging inwardly, stamps across to the door where she turns and hisses at James

Florence Ssssssssh!
James (*grandly*) Yes?
Florence (*fuming*) I'll *see you* as soon as possible if you don't mind!

Florence marches out through the door

Prudence (*airily*) Funny old trout, isn't she?
James (*embarrassed*) I—I . . . (*Pulling himself together*) And—now—to *work!* To work, shall we? (*Beaming at the "class"*)
"How doth the little busy bee
    Improve each shining hour."
(*Purring*) H'm?
Lionel (*flatly*) How *does* he?
James (*vaguely*) What?
Lionel The little busy bee—each shining hour—how does he improve it?
James (*testily*) How the hell should *I* know? Belt up, Birdwhistle (*Speaking generally*) "The James Tiller Crash Course on the Detection and Prevention of Crime" will now commence!
Lionel Ta-ra-re-*rah!*

James glares at him

James (*profoundly*) First we must ask ourselves—"What *is* crime?" (*Looking round, solemnly*) What—is—crime? (*Slight pause*) Crime *is*— and I quote . . . (*He makes to pick up a book from the desk. It is not there*) Er—crime is—and I quote . . . (*He is searching madly amongst papers on the desk*) And I quote . . . (*Fuming*) Who's been mucking about with my desk? (*Still searching*) And I quote . . . (*Fuming*) The damn thing was here a month ago. I know it was. I was quoting from it!
Lionel (*going to the desk and beginning to turn things over*) Can I help, Mr Tiller?
James (*roaring*) Don't interrupt me when I'm quoting!

Lionel opens a drawer in the desk and produces a bottle, a third filled with whisky

Lionel (*holding up the bottle*) Somebody's been quoting from this!
James Put that back! Er—we use that in the lesson dealing with "Drunkenness and how to detect it".
Lionel (*holding up the bottle again and looking at it*) Expensive lesson!
James Very. Pity the fees you paid don't cover it! (*He snatches the bottle*

from Lionel and returns it to the drawer) Now where's that damned . . . ?
(*Suddenly*) Ah! Here it is! (*From the drawer he takes a very small book.
To Lionel, beaming*) Thank you, Birdwhistle. You have been most help-
ful. You must be rewarded.

Lionel (*taking the bottle and holding it out to James*) Oh, thanks very much!
Just a little one. Just a *soupçon*!

James (*taking the bottle from him*) I shall personally write "Highly Com-
mended" on your "Passing-Out Diploma".

Lionel (*unenthusiastically* Thanks very much!

James (*after returning the bottle to the drawer*) And *now!* We will continue,
shall we?

Maggots Had we begun?

James (*after glaring at her*) First we must ask ourselves . . .

Lionel (*muttering*) What again?

James (*pontifically*) . . . *ask* ourselves "What is Crime?" (*He looks round
as before*) What—*is*—Crime? (*Pause, then solemnly*) Crime *is*—and I
quote an even greater authority than myself—(*he holds up the very small
book*) The Green Shield Stamp Handy Pocket Dictionary, which tells
us . . . (*He begins to fumble through pages*) Damn this small print!
Where are my glasses? (*Searching on the desk again*) Who's been mucking about with my glasses? (*Heaving things around on the desk*)

Lionel (*placidly*) Mr Tiller!

James (*barking*) Now what?

Lionel pats his own waistcoat pocket

(*Not understanding*) What?

*Lionel repeats the business. James automatically feels in his own waistcoat
pocket*

(*As he takes his glasses from his pocket*) Oh! I—I—er . . . ! (*Grudgingly*)
Thank you, Birdwhistle. Very perceptive!

Lionel Can I have my "Passing-Out Diploma" *now*?

James (*after glaring at Lionel*) Now attention, pupils! Having asked ourselves the profound question, "What is Crime," we find the answer—
(*holding up the book*)—here! (*Reading solemnly and slowly*) "*Crime is a
violation of the law!*" (*Looking at them all as if expecting applause*) And
there you have it—(*throwing the book on the desk dramatically*)—in a
nutshell!!

Lionel (*sarcastically*) Well, I never!

James (*enjoying himself—holding up his hand imperiously*) But . . . !
(*He automatically shoves his glasses up on his forehead*) But—having discovered that crime is a violation of the law, there is another question
we must ask ourselves!

Lionel "When are we going to learn something!"

James (*automatically and dramatically*) "When are we going to . . ." (*He
breaks off, flustered*) I—I—I . . . ! (*After glaring at Lionel*) We have to
ask ourselves—(*ponderously*)—What—is—the—law?

Maggots The law is an ass!

James A what?

Maggots An ass.

James (*grandly*) Not according to the—(*picking up the book again*)— *Green Shield Stamp Handy Pocket Dictionary*, it isn't!

Maggots (*muttering*) Charlie Dickens says it is.

James (*grandly*) I am not interested in the half-baked observations of one of your fellow Juvenile Delinquents!

Maggots But . . . !

James (*silencing her with a gesture*) "But me no buts!" (*Waving the book*) *The Green Shield Stamp Handy Pocket Dictionary* and *I*—will tell you what the law is. (*He is about to read, but again cannot find his glasses. Once more he is about to start ranting, but—very much aware of Lionel watching him—silently, but angrily, searches on the desk*)

Lionel (*after watching James for a moment or two—sweetly and quietly*) Coo-ee!

James looks up at Lionel. Lionel, with a beaming smile, gently taps his own forehead. James is puzzled. Lionel repeats the business. James's hand goes up to his own forehead, and, of course, finds the glasses. He is seething inwardly, but, without speaking, rams the glasses down on to his nose

(*Plaintively*) Surely I get my diploma *now*?

James (*reading loudly from the book*) *"LAW is a rule established by authority!"* (*Looking at the "class"*) You should be making notes of all this, y'know. However . . . ! (*Putting the book down*) And—laws established by authority should not be broken, *but*—(*solemnly*)—alas—and alack—they so often are!

Lionel T', t', t'!!

James Well may you "T', t', t'," Mr Birdwhistle!

Lionel Oh, thank you. (*Rapidly*) T', t', t', t', t'!

James (*after gulping*) There are numerous ways in which the laws of authority are broken daily. I want *you*—(*with sweeping gesture to "class"*) —to name some. (*Pointing to Maggots*) You!

Maggots (*promptly, and with meaning*) Taking money under false pretences!

James (*somewhat taken aback*) Er—quite right! We will deal with that later. (*Moving quickly to Prudence*) Prudence, my dear?

Prudence Soliciting.

James Er—quite right! Very wrong! (*To Lionel*) You!

Lionel Putting your head out of the carriage window when the train is in motion.

James's mouth opens, then closes. He points to Maggots again

Maggots *Murder!* (*She gestures shooting James*) Bang!

James nods his head approvingly and looks towards Prudence

Prudence Rape!

James (*shaken*) You have rather a—er—one-track mind. However—full marks! (*He looks towards Lionel*)

Lionel Pulling the Communication Cord for a lark. Penalty, Twenty Pounds.

James (*in spite of himself*) *Twenty?* Good God! Has it gone up to that? It used to be five!

Lionel (*with a shrug of the shoulders*) Well, there you are! Inflation!

James I must remember that the next time I . . . (*Then pulling himself together*) Er—I—I—I am somewhat amazed—nay, astounded that not one of you has mentioned the commonest crime with which the detective has to cope.

Lionel Ah, but we shan't be *common* detectives!

James (*warningly*) Birdwhistle!

Lionel *We* shall be—"Tiller-trained"!

James (*baffled*) Er—quite. Nevertheless, I would ask you to condescend to give your minds for a moment to the er—"trivial" but extremely prevalent crime of—theft.

Lionel Oh, yes, of course! Theft!

James (*dramatically*) *Theft!* (*Slight pause*) The taking of property which does not belong to you.

Lionel Very naughty!

James There is an old—er—Japanese proverb which says: (*He recites the following rubbish, or something like it, in a high-pitched voice*)
"Kwi quon shee tum long hoo yah,
  Soo fong pish me foo cha-cha,"
Which, translated into basic English, means—
"Him what takes what isn't His'n,
  Must give it back, or go to prison!!"
(*Then dramatically*) And, as fully-trained—*Tiller-trained*—detectives . . . it will be your . . . your *duty* to see that he *does!* (*And on the "does", he slaps his hand dramatically on top of the desk*)

Lionel (*carried away*) Where is he? (*Rising excitedly and looking around*) Where is he? Let me get my hands on him! (*Muttering to himself*) Kwi kwong kwi kum kwo kwak-kwak . . .

James Birdwhistle!

Lionel (*with a silencing gesture*) Keep your voice down! He'll hear you!

James (*louder*) *BIRDWHISTLE!!!!*

Lionel (*with a yelp of exasperation*) Aaaah! (*To James*) You see! He heard you! He's got away! *You'll* never make a detective!

James (*spluttering*) Wha-at?

Lionel You've no—what's the word?—*savoire faire.* No! That's *two* words. Er *finesse!* That's it! You have no *finesse.*

James (*fuming*) Finesse?

Lionel Finesse. Look it up in your "Old Moore's" dictionary.

James (*shouting*) *Sit down!*

Lionel (*with a start*) What . . . ? (*He runs a hand across his brow, then sits again. As he does so*) I got carried away!

James (*sadly*) Ah! If only that were *so!* (*Speaking generally*) Now! If I could have your undivided attention . . . ?

Prudence (*cooing*) You have mine, Papa!

James (*after reacting*) As "theft" is the commonest of crimes, we will make it the subject of our first lesson. Agreed? (*Before anyone can* *answer*) Agreed! There are, of course, many types of theft—and many types of thieves. High up on the list are the "master-minds", those genii who plan with meticulous—er—meticulation the big train robberies, the penetration of impenetrable bank vaults. But, we will for the moment, drop to the other end of the scale, where we find the riff-raff of the underworld—the small-time crooks, amongst whom we find the "dips".

Lionel The "dips"?

James So called because they—(*making a "dipping" gesture*)—dip.

Prudence (*her hand straying to her cleavage*) Er—where do they *dip*, Papa?

James (*aware of the position of her hand*) Yes, there as well; but mostly they prefer racecourses.

Prudence (*disappointed*) Oh!

Lionel Ah! I've got it!

James (*coldly*) Tell us what you've got, Mr Birdwhistle! That is, if it can be mentioned in mixed company.

Lionel When you say "dips" you mean pickpockets.

James When I say "dips" I mean "dips". There are the—the—well, shall we say—the *big* dips and the little dips.

Lionel Yes, lets! (*Reciting*)
"Big dips have little dips
Upon their backs to bite 'em
Those little dips have lesser dips
And so *ad infinitum*!"

James (*fuming*) Birdwhistle!

Prudence (*to Lionel*) Lovely, darling. You must recite it again, sometime.

Lionel (*immediately*) "Big dips have little dips . . ."

James Birdwhistle!

Prudence When we go upstairs, you can recite it then—with actions.

Lionel is unconsciously looking at Prudence's chest

Lionel Ooh! I can't wait to get at those dipping dippers!

Prudence coyly puts her hands over her bosoms

Prudence (*coyly*) Oh, Mr Birdwhistle!

Lionel (*in horror*) What? Oh, no, no! I didn't mean . . .

James (*roaring*) Can we get on?

Lionel (*flustered*) But I *must* explain. You see, she—(*indicating Prudence*)—though I meant her—her—(*he gestures vaguely*)—but I didn't! I meant —I meant . . .

James To clear Mr Birdwhistle's mind of all the obnoxious things he did, and didn't mean, we will ask him to give us a little demonstration.

Lionel (*apprehensively*) What of?

James Mr Birdwhistle will demonstrate just how the "Dip" dips!

Prudence (*her hands flying to her bosoms again—mock modest*) Oh, no! Not in public!

Lionel (*to James, alarmed*) But I've never "dipped"—not in public or anywhere else. I can't demonstrate.

James You can, and you will, *after* I have shown you how. *Now!* Stand up, Mr Birdwhistle—away from the others.

Lionel (*as he moves to the middle of the room; bashfully*) You're not going to make me look a fool, are you?

James (*approaching him*) That damage was done when you were first conceived. Now, stand up straight. You're not a question-mark. (*He straightens Lionel up by the shoulders*) Good heavens, man! When did your clothes last see their clothes-brush! (*He begins "dusting" Lionel's jacket with his hands—turning—almost spinning—him round in the process*) Look at them! Haven't been brushed since they said good-bye to the sports jackets at Montague Burton's. (*More "dusting"*) Disgraceful! (*He moves away a little from Lionel*) You really should buy yourself another suit, Birdwhistle.

Lionel I will, one day—when I win the Pools.

James (*with rather overdone blandness*) Short of ready cash, are we?

Lionel I don't know about you, but I'm short of any kind of cash.

James (*blander than ever*) Oh dear! We must do something about that!

Lionel (*almost in horror*) Oh, no, really. I couldn't allow you. (*In the same breath*) How much can you let me have?

James (*taking a wallet from his breast pocket and holding it almost under Lionel's nose*) Well, now—let me see.

Lionel (*placidly—seeing the wallet*) Oh! That's funny!

James What is?

Lionel Your wallet! It's just like mine!

James (*moving away*) Fancy that! (*He is thoroughly enjoying himself—and showing off. He winks to the girls*)

Lionel (*innocently*) Yes, but mine's got A PRESENT FROM BOGNOR REGIS on it.

James (*with "astonishment"*) Good heavens! How extraordinary! So has mine! (*More winking at the girls*) Well, well!

Lionel *Well, well, well!* Isn't that a coincidence?

James It is indeed! (*More winks*)

Lionel My Aunt Lottie sent me mine. Who sent you yours?

James (*approaching him again*) Your Aunt Lottie. (*He waves the wallet under Lionel's nose*)

Lionel Good lord! (*He looks at the wallet as if about to recognize it*) Then —*you* know my Aunt Lottie? Well! Isn't that amazing!

James (*beginning to get exasperated*) Birdwhistle . . .

Lionel It certainly is a small world!

James (*fuming*) I should like to see your wallet, Birdwhistle.

Lionel puts his hand towards his breast pocket, then draws it away

Lionel No, no! We might get 'em muddled!

James (*after gulping heavily*) Birdwhistle! Don't you *see*? Don't you *realize* what has happened? (*He waves the wallet again*)

Lionel Of course I do. My Aunt Lottie went to Bognor Regis last August, and she sent us both a wallet!

James (*beginning to crack up*) I—I—I . . .

Lionel Aunt Lucy went with her.

James whimpers and waves the wallet feebly

But *she* didn't send me anything, did she you?
James (*croaking*) Birdwhistle . . .
Lionel But perhaps you don't know Aunt Lucy?

James, without realizing, shakes his head wretchedly

Ooh! A proper old meany *she* is.

Completely broken, James can only make gurgling noises

I don't know why Aunt Lottie bothers to take her with her.
James (*almost sobbing*) Birdwhistle . . . (*Unconsciously, he goes down on one knee, still waving the wallet limply*)
Lionel They're going to Burnham-on-Crouch this year. Did you know?
James *Aaaaaaaaaaah!* (*It is a strangled cry of utter agony. With difficulty, he totters to his feet, and dementedly waves the wallet within a quarter of an inch of Lionel's nose. In strangled gasps*) *You—you . . . ! !* Hasn't it penetrated your thick skull yet? (*More frantic waving of the wallet*) This —this is—*your* wallet. *Yours, Man!! Yours!*
Lionel (*placidly*) Well, do you know, I thought it *must* be.
James (*babbling*) You *thought* . . . ?
Lionel (*still quite placidly*) Yes, 'cos you see, I *felt* you take it . . .
James (*babbling*) You felt me take it . . .
Lionel Yes, of course. Don't you remember you *said* you'd show me *how* to do it. Well, when you'd taken my wallet—shown me how to do it, well—I *did* it.
James (*babbling*) Did—what?

Lionel takes a wallet from his own breast pocket

Lionel (*holding it out; placidly*) This is yours, isn't it?
James (*hit right between the eyes*) I—I—I—I—I—I—I . . . !
Lionel (*looking at the wallet*) But it isn't a bit like mine. (*He unconsciously waves it in front of James's nose*)
James (*babbling*) You—you took—my wallet?
Lionel Wasn't I meant to?

James staggers away from him, a broken man

(*Politely*) Oh, Mr Tiller . . . ?

James stops in his tracks, then turns, facing Lionel. Lionel approaches him and gently returns James's wallet into his—James's —breastpocket. Then he, almost timorously, takes his own wallet out of James's hand

Thanks ever so much. (*As James is about to turn away*) Oh, Mr Tiller . . . ?

James gives an enquiring croak

(*Rather pleadingly*) If you *should* write to Aunt Lottie before I do—give her my love.

James totters to his desk and collapses into the chair behind it—shattered

(*Brightly*) Now! What happens next?

James (*in a loud hollow voice*) We will now have a short break—class dismissed for fifty-five minutes.

Lionel Dismissed?

James Yes. (*Gulping*) Playtime!

Maggots (*wildly*) Yipp-ee!

James (*in the same hollow voice*) You'll find the skipping ropes out in the hall.

Prudence (*cooing*) Mr Birdwhistle—are you interested in skipping?

Lionel (*with his eyes on James more than Prudence; babbling*) Well—er—no, not exactly. As a matter of fact I'm more interested in . . .

Prudence (*smoothly*) That's what I *thought*. But shall we get my bags upstairs first?

Lionel Your bags? Oh, your bags.

Prudence propels him towards her bags

Maggots (*following them; eagerly*) Then are you coming out to play?

Prudence (*turning and patting her on the head; tolerantly*) Don't be silly, child!

Florence appears on the landing

Lionel and Prudence—Lionel now carrying the bags and being propelled (rather reluctantly) by Prudence—move towards the staircase. They do not see Florence on the landing

Lionel (*not at all happy*) If you'd rather I took them up later . . .

Prudence (*coyly*) You are impatient! It won't take a minute; then we shall still have fifty-four minutes left.

Lionel (*alarmed, babbling*) But—I mean—I didn't mean—if you'd prefer some—fresh air . . . ! (*He stops at the bottom of the stairs*)

Prudence (*blithely*) No, no. I shall need that afterwards.

Prudence gives Lionel a little push forward, which causes him to stumble over the bottom step and fall headlong along the stairs, letting the bags go. Florence—unnoticed by them—has advanced to the top of the stairs

Lionel (*as the bags fall*) I'm so sorry. I—I—I don't know what's the matter with me. (*He picks up the bags*)

Prudence (*easily*) I do! You're too eager. There's plenty of time.

Lionel (*moving upstairs again, but with his head turned to Prudence as he speaks*) But—I'm not a quick worker. I—I'm always being told I'm—I'm too cautious!

Prudence Don't worry. We'll soon put that right.

Lionel (*now thoroughly alarmed*) But—but—but . . . (*He has mounted almost to the top of the stairs. He now turns his head and sees Florence looming over him. Very startled*) Aaaaaah! (*He lets the bags fall*)

Prudence is immediately behind him, so that when the bags fall down the stairs, she is not hit by them. Lionel, clutching the banister, stumbles backwards down the stairs. Prudence is compelled to do the same. Maggots rushes to the bottom of the stairs, somewhat alarmed. There is a state of confusion at the bottom of the stairs

(*Gasping, clinging to the banister, to Prudence*) I—I—I'm so sorry! So sorry! So sorry! It was—it was seeing—(*with a jerk of his head towards Florence*)—Mother Courage up there. (*Gasping*) Phew!

Florence descends the stairs slowly

Florence (*ominously*) What appears to be going on?
Prudence Nothing—yet! Mr Birdwhistle is taking my bags up to my room.
Florence Is he indeed!
Lionel Indeed I am.
Florence Very clever of you—seeing you don't know which one it is.
Lionel I—I—I . . .
Florence (*to Prudence; coldly*) You're in Number Ten.
Prudence Thank you.
Florence Next to mine.
Prudence (*flatly*) Oh!
Florence Yes (*significantly*) And I'm a very light sleeper!

After looking steadily at Prudence, then at Lionel, Florence moves off the stairs, allowing them to ascend. Lionel picks up the cases as he goes. Florence watches them. Very aware of this, they look down at her from time to time

Lionel (*to Florence*) Time me with your stop-watch!

Prudence and Lionel exit along the landing

Florence is still looking up at the stairs as Maggots gives her one of her sharp digs in the ribs with one finger

Florence (*giving a yelp of pain*) Aaah! (*Rubbing her side*) If you do that again, you young devil . . . ! What do you want?
Maggots Will *you* . . . ? (*She hesitates*)
Florence Will I what?
Maggots (*after looking at her*) On second thoughts—no! (*She moves across to the front of the desk*)

ames is still seated at the desk, with head bent forward, his hands almost covering his face. Florence goes to the other side of the room and begins a half-hearted search near the fireplace—for the jewels

(*Picking up a ruler from the desk, and tapping James's mortar-board with it*) Oi!

James slowly looks up—the picture of misery

Will *you* come out and play with me?

James lets forth a howl of misery

James (*burying his head in his hands again*) Go away! Go—*away!*

Maggots moves slightly away from the desk, and stands disconsolate for a moment or two

Maggots (*suddenly, in a raised, complaining voice, speaking generally*) I'm not *enjoying* myself here, y'know; not a bit!

A loud groan from James and a glare from Florence

I thought it was going to be ever such fun, but . . . (*Suddenly*) Oh! Look! (*She picks up Prudence's fur coat which she has left on the back of the chair she was sitting on*) Elizabeth Taylor's left her coat! (*Gaping at it*) Ooooh! Isn't it smashing? I expect she said good-bye to her honour when she got this!

Florence *What?*

Maggots Well, she didn't bring it with her! (*She drapes the coat around her shoulders*) Oooh! Isn't it marvellous! Ooh! It does things to you! (*She wiggles her hips*) It makes you feel all—(*she walks across the room in what she imagines to be a sexy way*)—all—voluptuous—carnal! (*She moves to the newel-post of the stair, and drapes herself against it, and sings in a low "Dietrich" growl*)
"Where have all the flowers gone?
  Long time passing.
  Where have all the flowers gone . . ."

James (*with a roar*) Get that potential "Lily of the Lamplight" out of here!

Florence (*rushing up to Maggots and tearing the coat off her*) Out!

Maggots (*flouncing to the door, then turning*) Y'know, I'd tell you two to get "with it" if you weren't past it!

Maggots flounces out through the door

James (*whimpering*) It's no use! It's no use! I can't go on.

Florence (*stroking the coat lovingly; vaguely*) What's the matter with *you*? (*She struggles unsuccessfully to get into the coat*)

James (*rising and striding up and down*) Everything! You—Soaker—those damn' jewels . . . !

Florence (*panting as she struggles*) That kid's right, y'know. This coat—it does do something to you.

James (*glaring*) It might—if you ever got into it!

Florence turns the coat upside down and drapes it round her

Florence (*as she drapes coat as far round her as it will go*) Ooh, yes! It makes you feel all . . . (*She growls sexily. She drapes herself against the newel-post and begins to sing in the "Dietrich" growl*)
"Where have all the flowers gone?
  Long time passing.
  Where have all the . . ."

James (*with a howl*) Is there a God?

Lionel appears almost at the run, on the landing. He is in a very dishevelled state. His hair is rumpled, his collar and tie half off, and his jacket only just on. One end of his shirt is pulled out at the front

Lionel (*as he appears*) Oh! Oh, my goodness!

Florence (*gaping at him*) What . . . ? (*She removes the coat*)

James (*roaring*) What the devil's the matter with *you*?

Lionel (*as he comes down the stairs*) Don't ask me! *Please* don't ask me! (*He covers his face with his hands, and in consequence, as he cannot see, almost falls down the stairs*)

Florence (*alarmed*) Aaaah!

James (*moving to the stairs*) Have you been fighting?

Lionel I'll say I have!

James What? What for?

Lionel My honour!

Florence (*grimly*) I hope you've still got it!

Lionel (*limply*) I think so!

James You'd better look and see. (*To Florence*) Flo! Leave the room!

Lionel Ooh! That female.

Florence What did she do?

Lionel I daren't think. But I only hope Mother doesn't get to hear about it! (*Noticing the coat in Florence's arms*) That's—that's *her* coat, isn't it? Miss Carlisle's?

Florence (*grimly*) It is!

Lionel Oh, Lordy, Lordy, she could do with that right now. She must be covered in goose-pimples!

Florence (*aghast*) Are you telling me she's up there—stark—starkers . . . ?

Lionel (*with a wail*) Don't ask me?

James (*eagerly*) Is she? Is she?

Lionel (*to Florence, indicating the coat*) Take it up to her, *please*!

Florence (*fuming*) I shall do no such thing.

Lionel But . . .

James (*with false indignation*) Of course my sister will not take it up. (*Taking the coat from Florence*) *That* will be *my* privi . . . er—duty!

Florence What?

Lionel (*anxiously*) Oh, no, Mr Tiller, you mustn't! You mustn't! Think of your honour!

Florence (*with scorn*) "*Think* of it?" (*Glaring at James*) He can't even *remember* it! (*She snatches the coat from James*) You'll stay where you are!

James But, Flo! Oh, Flo! Oh, Flo!

Florence Oh, no! (*Moving to the chair on which Prudence sat, and throwing the coat over the back of it*) If she wants it, she can come down and get it!

James (*rubbing his hands*) Now *that's* an idea. (*To Lionel*) Pop up and tell her that, will you? And tell her to come down right away! (*He moves behind the desk*)

Lionel (*unthinkingly*) Yes, Mr Tiller! (*He begins to run upstairs, then stops,* *horrified) What? (Realizing what he was about to do)* Aaaah! *(He scuttles down the stairs so quickly, he has to cling to the newel-post to save himself falling. During the next one or two lines, he notices something on the floor —hidden from the audience's view by the newel-post. He bends down and slowly picks up a leather bag. He quietly and slowly opens it)*

Florence moves to the front of the desk

Florence *(barking at James)* That creature leaves here at once, you understand?

James At once? Are you suggesting she goes to the railway station stripped to the buff? For God's sake! What is A.S.L.E.F. going to say about that?

Lionel has now opened the bag and taken out a piece of jewellery. He gives a yelp of surprise

Lionel *(gaping at the bag) Oh!* Oh, my goodness!

James *(glaring across at him)* Now what?

Florence *(seeing the bag in Lionel's hands, at once alert)* What have you got there?

Florence moves across to Lionel quickly, who holds out his hand, showing a piece of jewellery

(With a wild scream) Aaaaaah!

James *(roaring)* Flo, please—my head! *(He collapses into his chair and holds his head)*

Florence Oh, my *God*!!

She tries to snatch the bag, but Lionel draws it to himself

Lionel *(lightly slapping her outstretched hand)* Don't snatch! It's rude!

Florence *(wildly)* Give it to me!

Lionel No!

Florence Give it to me!

Lionel No! *(As he speaks he stamps one foot, which lands on Florence's foot)*

Florence *(in agony* Aaah! *(Trying to clutch her foot, which she cannot reach)* You—you . . . ! *(In agony, she hobbles across to the desk as quickly as she is able. To James, gesticulating and almost hysterical)* He's got 'em. He's GOT 'em!

James *(uncovering his face; irritably)* Who has? Birdwhistle? That was obvious from the first moment he arrived! *(Then, very alert)* "Got 'em"? Got what? *(With a yelp)* My God, you don't mean . . . ?

Florence *(wildly)* Of course I do! *(Rapidly)* He's got 'em! He's got 'em! He's got 'em!

James *(also rapidly)* Leave this to me! I'll get 'em! I'll get 'em! I'll get 'em!

James moves across to Lionel who is fingering the contents of the parcel

Now, Birdwhistle, Birdwhistle, Birdwhistle! What is it you appear to have . . . ?

Lionel holds open the bag for James to see. James at once makes to grab it, but Lionel is too quick for him

Lionel (*as he draws the bag away*) Aha! Lookee, lookee; notee touchee!

James is, for a moment, almost apoplectic, but pulls himself together, then moves away, laughing very falsely

James (*giving each "Ha!" its full value*) Ha! Ha! Ha! Ha! Ha!
Florence What?
James (*deliberately*) Ha! Ha! Ha! Ha! Ha! So they've turned up at last! Thank you, Birdwhistle! My sister and I have been searching for those for hours. Where did you find them?
Lionel They were at the bottom of the stairs, but—d'you mean they're yours?
James Of course they are! Who else would want such rubbish?
Lionel Rubbish? It looks genuine to me, and I should know. Mother was transferred to the jewellery counter at Woolworth's for a fortnight!
James (*with a wink at Florence*) Unless I am mistaken, you have in that bag a pendant formed by one large ruby, surrounded by diamond brilliants. Yes?
Lionel (*holding a pendant up*) Yes. You're right!
James (*witheringly*) What you are displaying is a pendant formed of one brilliant *diamond* surrounded by small *rubies*! Nevertheless . . . !

James approaches Lionel and, almost without Lionel realizing it, takes the pendant from him while talking

There should also be a necklace of forty-two graduated pearls.

James moves towards Florence and dangles the pendant in front of her. Florence, with a whimper, tries to snatch it from him, but James slips it into his pocket. Florence is furious and shows it. Lionel, meanwhile, searches in the bag

Lionel (*suddenly*) Yes! Here it is! (*Producing a necklace*) Necklace of—er —how many degraded pearls?
Florence (*barking*) Forty-two!
Lionel (*to Florence*) You've got a cold! (*Looking at the necklace*) Forty-two. I'd better check!

James moves near Lionel, who absent-mindedly hands him the bag

Hold this while I count, will you? (*Counting*) One, two, three, four . . . (*He continues counting*)

James almost snatches the bag and moves triumphantly towards Florence again

James (*under his breath to her*) Good old Soaker!
Lionel (*counting*) Nine, ten, eleven . . .
James Don't bother to count them! They're not worth it!
Lionel Not worth . . . ? Now you've made me lose count!
James I bought those at Marks and Sparks for one pound eighty.

62 Elementary, My Dear

Florence gives a long whimper

Lionel One pound . . . ?

James Eighty.

Lionel But . . .

James (*airily*) Props, my dear Birdwhistle! Props we use for instructional purposes; in Lesson Five, to be precise.

Lionel Lesson . . . ?

James Which deals with jewellery and the nicking thereof.

Lionel You mean—they really are—fakes!

James (*airily*) The fakiest of fakes! (*He begins to strew jewellery from the bag on to the floor as one would strew flowers*) Fakes! (*More strewing*) Fakes! (*And more*) Fakes!

Florence, gibbering with horror is darting hither and thither, picking up jewels

Lionel (*meanwhile*) I can't believe . . . !

James (*producing a jeweller's eyepiece from his waistcoat pocket and holding it out*) See for yourself, O thou of infinitesimal faith!

Lionel (*gaping at, but not taking the eyepiece*) What . . . ?

James (*very knowledgeably*) Used by the experts! Applied to the eye, so . . .

Florence approaches James, jewels in hand. James screws his eyepiece into one eye and takes a piece of jewellery from Florence

The bauble is examined thus . . . (*He looks through the eyepiece at the jewel, then cries out in horror*) Aaaaaah! (*He snatches another piece from Florence and examines it. More horror*) Aaaaaah!

Florence (*alarmed*) What . . . ?

James, making inarticulate noises, inspects another piece

James (*with a howl*) Oh—my—God!!

Lionel (*delighted*) I was right, Mr Tiller, wasn't I? They *are* real!

James staggers away. Florence follows him

James (*croaking*) Fakes! Fakes! The whole bloody lot!

Quick CURTAIN

SCENE 2

The same. Thirty seconds later

James, Florence and Lionel are discovered

Lionel is some distance away from the others, his back slightly turned to them. He is holding the pearl cluster up on one finger and is painstakingly counting the pearls. Florence and James are close to each other. James has a handful of jewellery. Florence has more in her hands. They are both just gaping at the "stuff". The chamois leather bag is on the desk

Lionel (*in a normal voice, counting slowly and solemnly*) Eleven, twelve, thirteen, fourteen, fifteen . . .

James (*turning irritably*) What the devil are you bothering to count those for? Haven't I told you . . . ?

Lionel Yes, I know you have, but—I can't believe . . . (*Petulantly*) Oh, Mr Tiller, I shall get cross with you. You've made me lose count again! (*He begins counting once more*) One, two, three, four . . .

Prudence, now wearing a bathrobe, appears on the landing—unnoticed by the others. She stops dead as, on looking over the banister, she sees them with the jewels

Florence (*somewhat hysterically*) James—are you *sure*? (*She speaks in a slightly lower voice, with Lionel in mind, but loud enough for it to be taken for granted that Prudence can hear*)

James (*testily, and also in a subdued voice*) Of course I'm sure! Was I ever wrong?

Florence (*tersely*) Yes!

Lionel (*counting*) Eleven, twelve, thirteen, fourteen . . .

Florence But surely Soaker . . . A hundred and fifty thousand . . . You said you knew they were worth at least that?

James Of course I did. And they are!

Prudence darts off along the landing

Florence (*getting rattled*) But you've just said they're—they're fakes!

James (*also getting rattled*) These, *yes*, but—but not *those*.

Florence (*baffled*) Those what?

James (*fuming, but quietly*) Those what Soaker brought. (*With a wail*) Oh, Gawd! My grammar!

Florence Then where did these come from?

James Gawd knows! Woolworths—MacFisheries!

Lionel (*counting*) Nineteen, twenty, twenty-one . . .

Florence (*after glaring towards Lionel, who still has his back to them*) How do you know Soaker hasn't . . . ?

Lionel (*without turning, calling suddenly*) Mr Tiller!

James swiftly claps a hand over Florence's mouth. She promptly bites it. James, silently registering pain, waggles his hand

James (*fuming as he crosses to Lionel*) What is it?

Lionel (*his eyes on a pearl*) There's a cracked one here.

James (*his eyes on Lionel*) There is indeed! Though I'm surprised you admit it!

Lionel (*innocently*) You knew?

James (*irritably*) Of course I knew.

Lionel (*innocently*) That's funny, 'cos I've just cracked it with my fingernail. (*Demonstrating*) Like this. (*Then*) Oh! Now I've cracked that one!

James (*baffled and fuming*) You—you—you . . . !

Lionel (*innocently*) They *are* fakes, y'know!

James (*fuming*) Didn't I say they were?

Lionel (*innocently*) Funny me coming across them—just like that.

James Just like what?

Lionel Well—lying on the floor, by the stairs. Yet you and Miss Tiller had been looking for them for hours, hadn't you?

James I—I—I . . .

Lionel Not very good "lookers", were you?

Florence They weren't by those stairs earlier on, that I'll swear!

Lionel Do you swear, too, Mr Tiller?

James Yes, I bloody well do!

Lionel (*shocked*) Oh, Mr Tiller, you've sworn—and in front of a lady! Well—your sister, shall we say?

James (*impatiently*) Now, look, Birdwhistle . . .

Lionel (*with hand to head*) I can't for the moment—I'm thinking!

James stamps angrily away

Florence (*to James, sotto voce*) Get him out of here!

Lionel (*suddenly*) Ah! I've got it! Mr Tiller, I've got it! Somebody hid these deliberately for one foul purpose!

Florence What foul purpose?

Lionel To sabotage Lesson Five!

James *What?*

Lionel That's the lesson you use them in, isn't it? Lesson Five; which deals with "Jewellery and the nicking thereof"!

James (*speechless*) I—I—I—I . . .

Lionel But who could have done such a—a dastardly thing?

Maggots enters from the hall, gently skipping with a piece of rope. She skips straight across the room and out through the open doorway

Maggots (*as she skips across the room, singing quietly*)
"My mother said,
   That I never should,
   Play with the gipsies,
   In the wood.
   If I did, then she would say . . ."

Maggots has gone

Lionel (*after Maggots has gone*) Could it have been . . . ? (*He looks towards the door. Then*) Mr Tiller, *I* am going to solve this mystery!

James (*gaping at him*) *You* are going to . . . ?

Lionel Yes, I am. (*Generously*) But you can help!

James can only burble

> (*Moving to and up the stairs*) Give me five minutes, that's all I ask; then we'll get to work!

James totters towards the desk

> (*On the landing, calling*) Mr Tiller!

James turns

> Catch! (*He throws the necklace to James, who, automatically, catches it*) You'll need that—Lesson Five!

Lionel darts off along the landing

James (*fuming as he moves behind the desk*) He's got to be disposed of! He's got to be disembowelled! (*He puts the necklace on the desk and picks up the memo pad*) He's got to be . . . (*Looking at the pad*) H'm! He's already down to be castrated! (*He sits at the desk*)

Florence (*frantically*) Never mind about Whistlebird! (*Rushing to the front of the desk and waving her cupped hands, full of jewels, in front of James*) What about these?

James (*roaring*) Don't loom over me! I can't stand it when you loom! (*He whimpers and puts his hands to his head*) Oh!

Florence (*almost dancing with anxiety*) But where did these come from? You've got to pull yourself together and think!

James groans

> (*Pleadingly*) James—Jamie Boy . . . !

James Oh, my God!

Florence Are you *sure* it isn't the stuff Soaker brought?

James (*leaping up from the desk and moving away*) Of course I'm sure! Are you daring to suggest that James Tiller doesn't know fakes when he sees 'em; or that Soaker doesn't?

Florence (*coming to him, still waving her cupped hands in front of him*) But supposing he's trying to do a double-cross?

James (*fuming*) What the hell are you talking about? (*Unconsciously waving his own cupped hands in front of Florence*) Who's he double-crossing? Himself?

Florence (*in a quavering voice*) But—Jamie Boy . . .

James (*clutching his stomach*) Drrrrh! Why should Soaker try to land me with a load of rubbish he knows I couldn't get him tuppence for?

Florence Then if it wasn't Soaker, who . . . ? (*Suddenly*) Oh, my God! (*She staggers a little*) Oh, my . . . ! I think I'm going to faint!

James What?

Florence (*staggering to a chair*) I've thought of something nasty!

James Then think of something nice.

Florence (*collapsing into the chair; weakly*) Water—get me some water—or *something*.

James (*moving to her*) Pull yourself together.

Florence Water—or *something.*

James We're out of "something"; it'll be water or nothing. (*He moves to a table and picks up a vase containing some rather aged flowers. He throws the flowers on the table and brings the vase to Florence, holding it out to her*) Here! Get this down you!

Florence (*about to take the vase, then leaping up*) That's right! That's right! Try to poison me now. But let me tell you something, James Tiller! If my nasty thought is right, you'll soon be trying to poison *yourself*!

James (*alarmed*) What? What are you . . . ?

Florence (*with satisfaction*) Ah! That's shook you, hasn't it? Yes! Got you right where the monkey got the whatever it was he did get, didn't it?

James burbles

(*In full spate*) If Soaker didn't bring those fakes here, then somebody else did. Right? (*Before James can speak*) Right! And—as nobody else has been here today, it must have been one of these so-called pupils of yours!

James (*in horror*) Oh, no, Flo; no, Flo; no, Flo; *no!*

Florence Those fakes are all replicas of the real stuff that Soaker was bringing. *Yes?*

James (*automatically*) Yes, Flo, yes, Flo, yes . . .

Florence Well, doesn't that strike you as funny?

James Not very. (*With a sigh*) Yet, I've always prided myself on my sense of humour.

Florence (*dramatically*) Somebody knew Soaker was bringing that stuff here today—and they planned to do a switch!

James (*with a loud gasp*) Good God, Flo! I believe you've hit it! Yes! *Yes, of course!* That's *it*! (*Patting her on the back*) Wonderful, Flo! A marvellous piece of deduction! (*Gazing at her in admiration*) Are you sure it wasn't *you* who wrote *The Mousetrap*?

Florence (*simpering with delight*) Oh, James!

Lionel's voice is heard, just outside the landing arch

Lionel (*off; loudly*) My dear Watson!

Immediately Lionel strides on to the landing. He is once more wearing his Sherlock Holmes outfit, complete with deer-stalker and spy-glass, etc.

James, on seeing him, gives a howl of horror

James (*a soul in torment, gibbering*) No! No! Oh, Gawd—no!

At once there is pandemonium. Lionel, the moment he gets to the centre of the landing, begins to pantomime playing a violin. As he does so, he "la-la's" the song, "Home on the Range", very loudly and slowly. Occasionally he breaks off the "la-la-ing" to sing the words. His rendering of "Home on the Range" might go something like this:

Lionel (*slowly*)
"La la la la la
La-la la la la la
Where the deer and the antelope play
Where seldom is heard
A discouraging word
La-la la la la la la la la.
(*Louder*)
HOME, HOME ON THE RANGE!
La-la la la la la la la la
Where seldom is heard
A discouraging word
La-la la la la la la la la . . ." (*Repeat as needed*)

James, almost immediately after seeing Lionel appear in the Sherlock Holmes outfit, goes near-berserk. With groans and howls be begins to move wildly around the room (ad lib.). After trying to climb a wall—unsuccessfully —he staggers towards the stairs as if to get at Lionel. Half-way up the stairs, he collapses with his arms on the banister, and head buried in his arms. He sobs noisily. Florence, during the above, follows James around trying to calm him down. When he goes up the stairs, she goes to the side of them, calling up pleadingly

Florence (*during the above business*) *James!* James! *Jamie Boy!* You mustn't—Jamie—I'm appealing to you. Think of your double rupture —*and* your varicose veins. *James*—it's your little sister Flo begging you . . . etc. etc.

James almost falls down the stairs and staggers to the chair behind the desk, obviously on the verge of apoplexy. He tears at his throat. Florence, hardly aware of what she is doing, looks round, sees the vase James used earlier, grabs it, rushes to James and puts it to his lips. James clutches the vase and drinks avidly

Florence (*suddenly, in horror*) Oh, Gawd! What have I done? (*She snatches the vase from James*)

Lionel suddenly stops "playing the violin", pulls himself to his full height, then calls

Lionel (*dramatically, loudly*) Watson!

James gives a little whimper, but looks towards Lionel—as does Florence

(*Again dramatically*) Quick, Watson! (*He pauses and raises a finger solemnly*) There's not a moment to lose! (*He runs along the landing and down the stairs at a terrific speed. As he does so he whistles like a falling rocket*)

Florence (*alarmed, rushing forward involuntarily*) Aaaah!

Lionel (*on arrival*) Speed, Mrs Hudson, speed! The essence of—well, you know what!

Florence (*fuming*) No, I don't—and my name isn't Hudson!

Lionel "A rose by any other name"—but the disastrous truth remains!

Florence Oooh!

Lionel (*moving to the front of the desk*) To work, Watson, to work! This case calls for all my skill—ingenuity—foresight—backsight—front-saddle—side-saddle . . .

James (*beating his forehead with the palms of his hands*) What the hell are you babbling about? (*Quickly*) And for God's sake don't tell me!

Lionel The case, Watson—*the case!*

James (*it is torn out of him, almost a scream*) *What effing case?*

Lionel (*calmly*) No, no! Not "The Effing Case". I cleared that up last week! Remember?

James can only gibber

(*Murmuring*) He was most—*most* grateful!

James (*gaping at him*) Who was?

Lionel Lord Effing, of course! Who else?

James (*demented*) Aaah!

Lionel But now we find ourselves faced with an even more devilish puzzle, Watson! "The Case of the Sabotaged Lesson!"

James The—the . . . (*He weeps*)

Lionel Lesson Five! (*He, very rapidly, produces his pen from his pocket and pantomimes giving an injection in the arm*) Sssss! (*As he is replacing the pen in his pocket*) Lovely breakfast! (*Striding around*) And now— the facts! The facts—what are they?

James (*fuming*) The fact as far as you're concerned is . . .

Lionel Wrong, Watson! Wrong—as usual! Now! You know *my* methods. We must apply them! (*Moving around*) Follow me, Watson!

James *What?*

Lionel beckons him peremptorily. James dazedly moves to his side

(*As he does so*) This isn't happening; it can't be.

Lionel (*near the staircase*) Aaah! (*He clutches James's arm*)

James (*shaken in spite of himself*) What, what, what, what?

Lionel (*pointing, dramatically*) There! By the staircase—at the very spot where the jewels were found!

James (*dazed*) What—where?

Lionel Here!

James Where?

Lionel There! (*He points to the carpet near the banister*)

James (*in disgust*) Grrrr!

Lionel (*dramatically*) That dark—(*down on his knees peering*)—dank stain! What can it be?

James Next door's cat! Bloody thing!

Florence (*moving to the stairs; grimly*) If you'll excuse me! I've had all I can stand of . . . (*She puts a hand on the banister*)

Lionel (*rushing to her, grabbing her hand and taking it off the banister*) Aaah! Fingerprints! Have a care, madam. In heaven's name, have a care! (*He is still clutching her hand*)

Florence (*with a scream*) James! Grab him before he . . . !

Lionel (*loudly*) Watson! Grab her before she does irreparable damage!

James (*singing dazedly and quietly to himself*)
"There's a land that is fairer than this—
And by grace we shall see it afar . . ."

Lionel (*releasing Florence*) Nothing must be touched—not until it has been tested!

Florence (*raging*) Well, God knows whether you've been tested, but you've certainly been touched!

Lionel (*dramatically*) Every little thing in this room, and—(*as he looks Florence up and down*)—believe it or not, that includes *you*—must be tested for fingerprints! *Now!* Watson! Have you got a—a—(*he searches for the word*)—a—a "whatsit"?

James (*blinking at him*) Of course I have!

Lionel A sprayer?

James (*haughtily*) That is *my* concern!

Lionel looks around the room quickly. His eyes light on a large pair of bellows, hanging by the fireplace

Lionel Ah! The very thing! (*He takes the bellows from the wall and crosses to James*) Watson! You know what to do with these! (*He thrusts the bellows into James's hand*)

James I know what I should do with 'em! (*He puts them aside*)

Lionel *Now!* (*Muttering to himself as he moves away*) Powdered graphite! (*He crosses to Florence*) Powdered graphite!

Florence (*gaping at him*) What?

Lionel I need powdered graphite!

Florence (*grimly*) I should have thought what you needed was syrup of figs!

Lionel (*dramatically*) Why am I thwarted at every turn? (*Suddenly grabbing Florence by the arm*) Flour! Have you flour in the kitchen?

Florence Course I have!

Lionel Get it! (*He moves away slightly*)

Florence (*fuming*) Now look here . . . !

Lionel *Flour!* Get it! (*Putting a hand on her arm*) Self-raising, of course!

Florence Oooh!

Lionel And for preference—McDougall's!

Florence (*clutching her head*) I—I . . .

Lionel And we must remember—all of us—from now on, not a finger must be laid on anything. *Anything!* Understand? There must be no touching of furniture; no handling of knick-knacks!

James (*to Lionel, under his breath*) Steady! Steady! (*Indicating Florence*) Er—mixed company!

Lionel (*as he moves to the desk*) Every ornament in this room might reveal a tell-tale fingerprint. (*He picks up a silver-plated inkstand from the desk*) This inkstand, for instance . . . (*Twisting it round in his hand*) We shall soon know who has handled this! (*Replacing the inkstand and picking up a paper-knife*) And whose criminal prints shall we discover here?

(*Replacing the paper-knife and scooping all the jewellery into his hands. Running the jewellery through his hands*) But *these*! (*He drops a piece of jewellery on to the floor. Casually*) Pick that up, Watson.

James (*fuming*) I—I . . . (*But he stoops to pick it up*)

Lionel But for heaven's sake, man—don't touch it!

James leaps away from the jewellery

(*Still running jewels through his hands*) These will tell us most of all! See how they sparkle! Like a silver moon on a placid sea!

Prudence appears on the landing—unnoticed by the others. She is now wearing leather—black—tight trousers and jerkin. She has a small revolver concealed in her hand

Yet somewhere on the scintillating surface of each and every piece there may be a damning print of guilt waiting—waiting to be revealed! *So! What do we do? What do we do?*

James (*fuming*) What we do is . . .

Prudence (*in a hard, rasping voice*) Save your breath, Papa! I'll tell him!

There is a hubbub for a moment as James, Lionel and Florence spin round

James (*as he does so*) What? What? What?

Florence Aaaah!

Lionel Mrs Moriarty! (*He drops the bag on to the desk*)

Florence, in panic, immediately faces the audience and begins to sing wildly

Florence (*singing*) "La Donne e Mobile", etc.

Lionel rushes to her side and joins in the singing

James (*roaring at them*) Shut up!

Lionel immediately stops. Florence does not. Lionel claps a hand over her mouth. Florence bites it and stops singing

Lionel (*in pain*) Aaaaah! (*He wags his hand*)

James (*to Lionel, furiously*) I told you to stop singing! (*To Prudence*) What the devil game do you think you're playing?

Prudence (*still on the landing*) Same as you, Papa! But I'm making a better job of it!

Florence (*rushing to James's side; wildly*) Didn't I tell you . . . ? Didn't I say . . . ? Those were my very words! You can't deny it, can you? And wasn't I right?

James (*roaring at her*) Belt up!

Prudence Yeh! And that goes for you, too!

James (*roaring*) What? Why, you cheap little . . .

Lionel (*rushing behind James and muttering*) Careful, Watson! Careful! Remember my motto, "Play it cool!"

Prudence The Farndale sparklers, Papa; the ones Soaker left here this morning. *I want 'em!*

Lionel (*babbling*) The Farndale sparklers? (*Moving to the desk and picking up the bag*) But you can't possibly mean . . . ?

Prudence I mean what I say, Birdy-Boy! It's a nasty habit I've got into! Now, I'm coming down these stairs and you are going to put them right into my hand.

Lionel (*blinking*) The stairs?

Prudence (*snapping*) The sparklers! You'll give them to me—*or else!* (*To James*) And I don't like *alternatives*, Papa; they can be rather messy!

James (*burbling*) I—I—"sparklers"—I—I—don't know what you're talking about!

Prudence No?

James No. (*To Florence, with assumed airiness*) Flo, do *you* know what she's talking about?

Florence I—I . . . (*Faintly*) Water—or something.

James (*moving to Lionel*) Do *you* know what she's . . . (*In disgust*) No, of course you don't? *You* don't even know what *you're* talking about! (*He turns and speaks to Prudence, pompously*) Er—Miss—er—Carlisle —should that really be your moniker . . .

Prudence It isn't—but go on.

James Er—having gone into "committee"—at great length and considerable wastage of precious time, we have reached the unanimous decision that we are completely and utterly unaware of—of . . . (*He is lost. Irritably*) What the hell are we completely and utterly unaware of?

Prudence (*practically*) What I am talking about.

James (*gratefully*) Thank you! Thank you! Most kind!

Prudence Not at all! But—we'll take it for granted, shall we, that *I* know what *I'm* talking about? *And* you'll hand that stuff over without further shananakin or . . .

Prudence suddenly, but calmly, reveals the revolver in her hand. The others react

I did say alternatives could be messy, didn't I?

James (*wiping his brow with his handkerchief; to the others, with assumed jocularity*) Now, now, keep calm! Don't lose your heads! You realize, of course, she's only joking!

Lionel (*relieved*) Oh, is she?

James Yes! (*To Prudence*) Aren't you?

Prudence (*calmly*) Am I?

James Of course you are! Very funny! (*He "laughs"*) Ha! Ha! ha! (*He motions others to "laugh" also*)

Florence (*heavily*) Ho! Ho! Ho!

Lionel (*tremulously*) He! He! He! (*Then singing, unconsciously*) "Little brown jug don't I love . . ." (*He breaks off, miserably. To Prudence*) You are—(*he gulps*)—j-joking, aren't you?

Prudence (*almost casually*) I wonder if I am? (*She nonchalantly points the revolver towards the mantelpiece and fires. A large ornament is immediately shattered*) Apparently *not!*

The others stand frozen with horror

So . . . ! (*She waves the revolver at all of them in turn*)

James, Lionel and Florence, with yelps of alarm, move into action. Lionel disappears behind the desk. Florence crouches by the armchair. James flattens himself out on the floor in front of the settee. Prudence runs quickly down the stairs

(*As she does so, very business-like*) Come on! On your feet, the lot of you! (*To James, brandishing the revolver*) You! (*Likewise to Florence*) And you!

James and Florence rise quickly. James immediately puts his hands up. Florence follows suit

(*Looking round*) Where's . . . ? (*Moving to the front of the desk*) Come on, Birdy-boy! Show yourself!

Lione's head comes slowly up from behind the desk. His deer-stalker which was on his head correctly, has now slipped round so that the flaps are over his ears once more. He slowly comes to his feet. He still has the chamois leather bag in his hand

Now! Hand over! (*She holds out a hand*)

Maggots comes in from the door and quickly takes in what she imagines to be the situation

Maggots (*indignantly and loudly*) Oooh! You mean things! You've started again without *me*! (*She goes to stand beside James and, seeing his hands above his head, puts her hands up likewise*)

James (*from the corner of his mouth*) Go away!

Maggots What?

James Beat it!

Maggots Shan't! Unless I get my money back! (*With a jerk of her head towards Prudence*) What's she pretending to be?

Prudence (*still pointing the revolver at Lionel*) I'm waiting, Birdy-Boy!

Maggots (*to James*) What's she waiting for?

Lionel (*babbling*) But—but—Miss—Miss . . .

Prudence Just call me Dora—*Diamond Dora*.

James (*with a yelp of alarm*) Oh, my God! Diamond Dora!!!

Florence (*with a wail*) Oh, *no*!

Prudence (*half turning to James*) Rings a bell, does it?

James (*wretchedly*) A very cracked one! (*Gaping at her*) Diamond Dora! You! I can't believe . . . !

Prudence Just you hang on a second and I'll convince you. (*Turning to Lionel*) I'm still waiting, Birdy-Boy!

Maggots (*enthusiastically*) Ooh! Isn't she good! Is it my turn next?

Lionel (*babbling*) But, Miss—Miss—Dora Diamond—I assure you you're quite mistaken. These—jewels—(*holding up the bag*)—they're—they're utterly—price—less.

Prudence Sure they are! I wouldn't be after 'em if they weren't!

Lionel (*babbling*) No, no, you misunderstand. I don't mean they're priceless. I mean they're priceless. (*Groaning*) Oh dear!

Prudence I know what they're worth! Think I'd hop into bed with a drunken sot like Soaker if I didn't?

James (*with a yelp*) *What?* You hopped into bed with—with *Soaker?*

Prudence Sure I did! On the chance of picking up a hundred and fifty thousand quids' worth of "stuff", I'd even hop into bed with *you!*

Florence (*in disgust*) *Oh!*

Maggots (*to James*) Bet she *wouldn't*—not in real life!

Prudence Soaker was shooting off his mouth off in a pub a month ago, about some big job he was going to pull off.

Florence (*lowering her arms and shouting across at James*) Didn't I tell you . . . ? Didn't I say . . . ? Soaker . . . Those were my very words! You can't deny it, can you? And wasn't I right?

Prudence (*pointing the revolver at Florence*) Pipe down, Flossie!

Florence (*after putting her hands up quickly*) *Flossie!*

James (*to Prudence*) And Soaker told *you* about . . . ?

Prudence About the Farndale jewels—and that he was bringing 'em down to you? Yep! Why else would I be here?

James (*with a roar*) The stupid, half-witted, sex-starved . . . ! (*Slowly and with magnificent restraint*) I shall have to speak to him!

Prudence Mind you, it took a whole bottle of Scotch and a generous helping of "Heigh-ho, Come-to-the-Fair" in a feather bed, to get it out of him—but I got it!

Maggots (*to James*) *What's* she talking about? What's "Heigh-come-to-the-fair"?

James Er—it's a new deodorant that's just come on the market!

Lionel suddenly comes from behind the desk. He is incensed

Lionel (*coming near Prudence; very indignantly*) Now listen to me! I've heard some incredible things said this afternoon, and I've been silent far too long!

James No, you haven't.

Lionel (*to Prudence*) Miss Diamond, are you telling me that you actually are a notorious jewel thief?

Maggots (*to James*) He's good, too, isn't he?

Prudence I'm telling you nothing, Birdy-boy—except—to hand over that bag—(*suddenly pushing the revolver into Lionel's stomach*)—right now!

Lionel completely ignores the revolver pressing into him

Lionel And as for *you*, Mr Tiller . . . ! I don't know what to say to you!

Prudence (*sticking the revolver in his stomach*) Birdy-boy . . .

Lionel (*ignoring the revolver; to James*) Am I to understand that you are —a hedge?

Prudence (*pushing the revolver further into his stomach*) Birdy-boy . . .

James (*to Lionel*) A *what?*

Lionel I mean—a "fence". A receiver of stolen property?

Prudence (*menacingly*) Birdy-boy, Diamond Dora has got to have . . .

Lionel (*irritably*) Oh, do be quiet! "Diamond Dora has got to have", indeed! From what I've just heard, Diamond Dora has already *had*!

Prudence You don't like me very much, do you?

Lionel No, I do not! Furthermore, I am allergic to feather beds! (*To James*) Mr Tiller, I can't believe—and after what you said to us about people who take other people's belongings!

James I—I . . . What did I say? I can't remember.

Lionel I'll tell you exactly what you said! "Kwish kwash kwisoo long fee fee—hong lee too song pish hee hee." *That's* what you said!

Prudence (*suddenly losing her temper*) Are you going to hand over the stuff or do I have to shoot the lot of you?

Florence (*to Lionel, in a panic*) For God's sake, give 'em to her!

Lionel (*innocently*) But she doesn't want *these*. She wants . . .

James (*suddenly, loudly and excitedly; pointing*) My God! Holmes! Look! There!

All look round, startled

Lionel (*moving from Prudence a little; excitedly*) What? (*Looking round*) Where, Watson, where?

James leaps across to Lionel and snatches the bag from his hand

(*Dazed*) What—what . . . ?

James puts the bag into Prudence's hand, then dashes up to the chair and gets her coat

Prudence (*gaping at the bag in her hand, then at James*) What the hell's going on?

James Your coat. (*He slips it over her shoulders and begins leading her towards the hall*) I take it you'll be leaving us now?

Prudence (*stopping at the entrance*) That was very clever of you, Papa! And very wise!

James (*beaming at her*) From such an expert—praise indeed! May I quote you in my brochures? (*After a quick look towards Florence, drawing Prudence close to him*) And—er—are you in the phone book?

Florence (*booming*) James!

Prudence, with a smile, kisses one of her fingers, touches James's lips with it, then exits to the hall

Florence (*fuming*) If that woman ever shows her face here again . . .

James (*leaving the archway*) I don't think she will, but—if she should— we'll be prepared. (*He lightly tosses Prudence's revolver into the air and catches it again*)

Florence (*gaping*) What . . . ? You . . . ?

Lionel Mr Tiller! You—you took her revolver?

James (*airily*) Just a keepsake!

Maggots (*loudly*) I wish somebody would tell me what's going on!

Lionel (*to James*) And you've let her go off with a load of fake jewels?

James Why not? *She* brought 'em!

Lionel She . . . ?

James Who else? She was obviously going to plant 'em in place of the real ones. (*To Florence*) They must have dropped out of her coat pocket when you were trying to pour yourself into it—the coat, not the pocket.

Maggots (*louder*) I wish someone would tell me . . .

Lionel (*to James*) Then the—the Farndale jewels—you *have* got them?

James I—er—I . . .

Lionel And you *are* a crook—a fence! (*Looking towards Florence*) Both of you! Two crooked fences! (*He moves away*)

Florence (*tremulously*) James . . . !

Lionel (*striding up and down stage*) If I'd known that! If I'd known that . . . (*Stopping up stage*) And the jewels—where are they now?

James (*pacing up and down stage*) If I knew that! If I knew that!

Maggots (*loudly*) I wish someone would tell me . . . !

Lionel (*excitedly*) Of course! I see it all now! That nun—Mother Karate Soaker! She brought them, didn't she?

Florence (*excitedly*) Say "No", James!

Maggots (*suddenly crossing towards the hall*) Well, if nobody's going to tell me anything, I'm going! (*She picks up her hat, which has been on the table below the archway from the beginning of Act I, Scene 2, and puts it on her head*)

Florence (*alert*) What? Where are you going?

Maggots For a walk—to find the police station.

James
Florence (*in great alarm*) *What?* } Speaking together

Maggots Might want to call there later on! (*Chirpily*) See you! (*She moves to the archway, then turns. To Florence*) Oh, and I want *three* poached eggs for my tea—*or else!*

Maggots exits

Florence (*moving quickly towards the hall*) Come back! Come back, you little horror, or . . . (*She suddenly lets out a loud scream*) Aaaaaaaaaaah!

James What the *hell* . . . ?

Florence (*pointing to the table below the arch; hysterically*) There! There! On the table . . . ! (*She totters. Moaning*) Water—water—or something! (*She totters again*)

A small chamois leather bag is on the table. James and Lionel both rush towards the table. They collide half-way there, sort themselves out, then proceed. Lionel reaches the table first and grabs the small chamois leather bag

James (*almost on him*) No, you don't!

Lionel Yes, I have! (*He evades James to the middle of the room and looks into the bag*) And they are! Look! (*He holds out a piece of jewellery*)

Florence (*excitedly*) Get 'em, James! Get 'em!

James charges bull-like at Lionel who sidesteps adroitly. James, unable to stop, charges on and collides with the suit of armour which collapses on to the floor

(*In horror*) Aaaah!

James, clutching his head and moaning, turns

Lionel I can't let you have these, Mr Tiller. I can't, really. It wouldn't be fair—to you. Your feet must return once more to the straight and narrow. (*Looking at James's feet*) They're terribly broad at the moment!

James (*roaring*) Birdwhistle!

Lionel No! You shan't have them! You shan't! And to show you I mean it . . . (*He very quickly drops the bag on to the floor and immediately begins jumping on it*)

James (*roaring*) No! No! Oh, my *God*!!

Florence (*screaming*) Aaaaaaah! (*She covers her eyes*)

Lionel (*giving a final jump*) There! (*He moves towards the hall*)

At once, James and Florence rush to the bag, get on their knees. James snatches up the bag—it is now a paper one

James (*gaping*) What the . . . ? (*He dives his hand in the bag*) Aaaah!

Florence What . . . ?

James (*extricating his hand from the bag and looking at it*) Butterscotch!

Lionel (*calling happily from the archway*) Coo-ee!

James and Florence, still on their knees, look at him. Lionel dangles the chamois leather bag between a finger and thumb

James (*with a roar, struggling to his feet*) Why you . . . ! ! !

James and Florence rush towards Lionel, but stop suddenly as Lionel suddenly produces Prudence's revolver and smilingly threatens them with it

Lionel (*warningly*) A-ha!

James (*gaping at the revolver*) What—what . . . ? (*He slaps his jacket pockets, then, with a howl*) My God! You—you took . . . ?

Lionel (*fires, another ornament smashes on the mantelpiece. Tossing the revolver lightly into the air and catching it again, beaming at James*) Er . . . just a keepsake!

Quick CURTAIN

FURNITURE AND PROPERTY PLOT

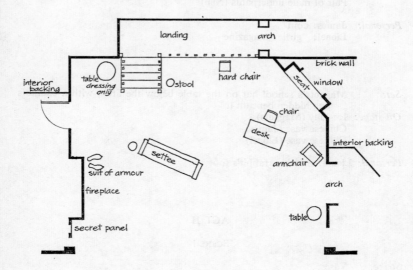

ACT I

SCENE 1

On stage: Settee. *On it:* cushions

Armchair. *On it:* cushion. *Down one arm:* bra, panties, tights

Hard upright chair

Window-seat

Stool

Desk chair

Large desk. *On it:* telephone, silver-plated inkstand, paper-knife, writing materials, "RING AND ENTER" card, newspapers, sheets of paper, list of visitors, notebook, pad, dictionary, ruler. *In drawer:* bank "change" bag, bottle of whisky. *Beside it:* waste-paper basket

Occasional table (below arch)

Occasional table (beside settee) *On it:* vase with fading flowers

Suit of armour

On mantelpiece: clock, ornaments (to be broken)

By fireplace: poker, pair of ornate bellows

On wall behind desk: medieval chastity belt

Off stage: Duster (**Florence**)
Fibre suitcase, binoculars, camera (**Lionel**)
Chamber-pot (**James**)
Braces (**James**—for "lifting" from Lionel)
Deer-stalker hat, meerschaum pipe with half a cigarette in it, spy-glass, Biro pen (**Lionel**)
Duffle bag (**Maggots**)
Pair of male underpants (**Nun**)

Personal: **James:** coin
Lionel: "girlie" magazine

SCENE 2

Set: **Maggots's** school hat on the table below the arch, with a chamois bag hidden beneath it
Off stage: Ice-lolly (**Maggots**)
Chinese vase (**James**)
Chinese vase (**Lionel**)

Personal: **Lionel:** matches, rabbit's foot

ACT II

SCENE 1

Strike: Vases

Set: Leather bag behind newel-post, containing pieces of jewellery including pearl necklace

Off stage: Handbell (**James**)
Mortar-board and gown (**James**)
2 expensive suitcases (**Prudence**)

Personal: **James:** spectacles, wallet
Lionel: wallet, jeweller's eyepiece

SCENE 2

Off stage: Rope (**Maggots**)
Revolver (**Prudence**)
Paper bag (**Lionel**)
In secret panel: box of Black Magic chocolates
Carpet, with patch of dust on it
Stair carpet
Window curtains

LIGHTING PLOT

Property fittings required: pendant, wall-brackets (dressing only)
Interior. A lounge-hall. The same scene throughout

ACT I, Scene 1. Midday
To open: General effect of spring mid-morning light
No cues

ACT I, Scene 2. Midday
To open: As previous scene
No cues

ACT II, Scene 1. Early afternoon
To open: As previous scene
No cues

ACT II, Scene 2. Early afternoon
To open: As previous scene
No cues

EFFECTS PLOT

ACT I

SCENE 1

Cue 1	**James:** ". . . the House of Lords!" *Telephone rings*	(Page 9)
Cue 2	**Lionel** exits *Telephone rings*	(Page 23)
Cue 3	**James:** ". . . quite elementary!" *Sound of noisy car approaching*	(Page 23)
Cue 4	**Maggots:** "It's my brother!" *Carhorn blares*	(Page 24)
Cue 5	**Maggots:** ". . . tear this place to pieces!" *Screech of brakes*	(Page 24)
Cue 6	**Lionel:** "But, listen . . ." *Door slam*	(Page 25)

SCENE 2

No cues

ACT II

SCENE 1

Cue 7	**Florence:** "You were . . ." *Handbell clangs*	(Page 41)
Cue 8	Lionel rises to his feet *Handbell clangs*	(Page 41)

SCENE 2

No cues